Praise for Score Selling™

"Our goal was to increase our market exposure through a more focused and accountable sales process that increased closed business. Score Selling™ provided results of average gains in individual professional productivity of 15-20% over the year. I highly recommend Score Selling™ to any organization seeking to improve sales results in their organization."
--John Clark, President at Signal Energy Constructors a Barnhart Company

"Score Selling is the best sales training solution I have ever employed, bar none. In the first phase of the program we tracked pipeline growth of 44% which is $25.7 million added to our deal pipeline. Our results were well beyond our expectations. I found it excellent for the following;
Sales Assessment -- The Score Selling Assessment was an extremely important first step for us. Many of our salespeople are veterans, while some were brand new. Additionally, the Parts and Service Rep has a different dynamic and objective than our Machine salespeople. The Assessment helped us a lot in identifying their needs and Kevin helped us map those needs into a custom fit sales training program.
Sales Training -- The Training program itself was excellent. Kevin engaged and challenged our salespeople to participate and apply the training in the field. In the past, Industry sales trainers would spend a lot of time speaking about industry insider information and we already have the finest in product and industry training from our manufacturers and trade groups. Score Selling, on the other hand, isolated the SALES issues which were keeping our salespeople from competing in more deals. We came away with new methods to build rapport and good questions to strengthen relationships while being able to deal with the objections of price, availability, current vendor and feature set. Our salespeople have new approaches to refocus the customer on the application and establish and protect our value in the deal.
Sales Tools -- the Score Selling sales tools were essential to our salespeople learning and applying the information. We employed both the time management tools and we are now deploying the CLIENT Map opportunity profile.
Sales Call-Days -- These training days alternated each hour of training with an hour of the sales team splitting up and making phone calls, before reconvening to review results and train again. This was extremely effective

particularly when the team learned to make calls on executives who were typically higher in the organization than the level at which our salespeople were used to calling. Our team made 2,065 phone calls, achieved 146 CEO referrals and set 123 new meetings.
Online Training Preparation and Reinforcement -- the program has an accompanying online component so that our sales team showed up prepared for the training.
Management Reporting -- We were able to see where our sales team was in the program, who was participating, who was leading and who needed some additional assistance. We came away with a framework installed into our management reviews with the salespeople which is helping to keep our deal awareness and participation levels high.
I highly recommend the Score Selling program to any lift truck company serious about growing sales revenue from new opportunities.
--Brian Hamilton, General Manager Georgia Operations, Thompson Lift Truck Company

"With over 25 years in sales and sales training I have seen countless "Selling Systems", but Score Selling™ is the first I have encountered that provides a comprehensive system for organizing the territory to ensure maximum time management as well as sales performance...To make it simple, if you have a sales force and want to help them increase their efficiency and create greater revenue, employ this system."
--Les Berry, District Sales Manager, Parts Associates, Inc

"Having a call template that enables me to counter objections concisely and quickly allows me to talk more naturally and confidently from the beginning of a call. The confidence of knowing what to say gives me the edge to be more aggressive in my sales. Would I recommend the training to others? YES, the training allows the novice salesperson to over come their fears of "selling". I have 20 years of experience, but sales calls always intimidated me. The training allowed me to minimize that anxiety and approach my sales days with greater confidence."
--Brian Dooley, Account Manager, Financial Industry

"We began using Score Selling sales training solution about 4 months ago and during this time we have successfully implemented the prospecting, lead generation and time management portions of his program. We have completely overhauled our sales messaging, fully dialed in our approach to a new level

and experienced gains beyond the goals that were established at the beginning of the program. We implemented the executive level calling with fantastic results; the voicemail campaign; and the compression prospecting Call Day. In this short time period our prospecting pipeline has almost doubled (48%). I attribute this success to the Score Selling™ model that Kevin has provided. If you are a single sales person or manage 100 sales people, I would strongly urge you to look at Score Selling as a tried and proven system to help you exceed your sales goals. Your sales team will find Kevin to be a true asset."
--Curt Dowling, Senior Vice President, Benise-Dowling Associates

"I had the opportunity to participate in Kevin's Score Selling program. Without a doubt, it was one of the better Sales Training programs I have taken over the years. Kevin was a very knowledgeable and enthusiastic presenter which I believe provided significant benefit to the sales process. I would highly recommend the Score Selling program."
--Bob Walters Strategic Account Manager, Kliklok-Woodman

"Kevin is a great trainer."
--P.G., Heavy Equipment Sales

"I can sell more after being in Score Selling™ Sales Training because I now have a better overall picture of the opportunity and how to collect/ use information and what questions to ask, when to listen and when to attack, identify/prioritize opportunities."
R L., Controls Product Manager, Heavy Equipment Sales

"He made the class fun. Which in turn makes it easy to learn.
-- Waylon. F., Territory Sales Specialist

"I met Kevin as a result of my employer hiring him as a consultant to examine, review and study the present methods of Selling being used at the company. Kevin, is very unique and best of all he is truly a "Been there, Done That and has been very Successful" as a Sales Representative. He implements an intense dialogue to examine and methodically review, critique and implement action plans to increase the individuals sales reps and company's bottom line. I personally recommend Kevin based on two things; the man has Integrity of Character and his Score Selling™ program works. Score Selling™ is genuinely unique and not a copycat. The methodology

examines and tracks time management and timed results with emphasis on systematic ready to use recordings of all parts of Sales efforts. Truly, I could accurately keep "Score" of my Goals, Efforts and Results. My confidence and time management greatly improved. Highly Recommended for anyone in sales, networking and requiring face time with clients/ customers."
--Jason Konas, Commercial Construction Sales

"I commend Kevin on his professionalism and his ability to take on many roles during our sessions. With our sometimes eclectic group it's not enough to be a trainer you have to also be a student, pacifist, encourager and have a great sense of humor."
--Manny Campbell, Strategic Account Manager, Kliklok-Woodman

"I feel more comfortable with objection handling and will use those skill sets more effectively." Bryan F, Territory Sales
"Score Selling™ helps me to sell more by following the rule of CLIENT™ and LANC™ much more closely, do a better job qualifying, and build org charts. It emphasized where I need to be more organized and how I can better gather intelligence and be a better communicator."
--John Z. Project Specialist, Industrial Sales

"I set realistic, measurable and attainable goals. It taught me to always know what our $$$ goals are and to offer "Fries" with every order. Also to remind customers about the programs we are offering."
--P. Parker, Sales Leader

"I believe Score Selling has allowed me to look at sales from outside the "box". This is more or less my first job with direct exposure to sales. Therefore, most of my sales training (before Score Selling) has been geared primarily toward the old way of doing things. This has not been a bad thing, however, Score Selling has allowed me to concentrate my pitch toward offering the prospect a solution to their problems versus a list of the services (value added or otherwise) we have to offer. I truly believe most prospects goal is to obtain solutions to their problem."
--Barry M., Account Manager, Credit Industry

"Score Selling™ Sales Training equips me to sell more by the CLIENT™ approach. I believe it will be essential for all the sales team to have a better vision of the clients needs and improve customer relationship."
--R.S., Sales Engineering Supervisor, MFG Sales

"Great Learning Experience. I learned to be listening and working on available options to overcome objections. After every call, evaluating how to improve."
--J. Wilson, Sales Specialist

"I found it very valuable to see in writing all of our strengths as a company; all of our advantages over other companies and I will use that to try to sell more and to close sales more quickly."
--T. Smith, Territory Sales

"We had been involved in ScoreSelling training for a few months and we decided to have a training session where we would each work the phones using what we had learned, record our results and then reconvene to discuss our progress. During our second session I was making my calls with some good results but I had reached a prospect on my list that I had called before. On my previous call to this gentleman, he had very firmly insisted that I never call him back. About this time Kevin walked into my office and asked how it was going. I told him about the next call on my list and that he had told me to never call again. Kevin asked me what I planned to do and I said I was going to call him anyway. After a few minutes of discussing this situation Kevin suggested that this gentleman may just be a bottom line kind of guy so maybe we should just cut straight to it. We had been practicing many techniques in our course so I just jotted down a few notes to prep this next call...
I dialed his company number and asked to be transferred to Bill. I thought I would probably get his voicemail but unexpectedly he answered "This is Bill". I said "Bill, you don't know me but I work with Benise-Dowling National Painting and we have painted the exteriors of 30 Embassy Suites and have been able to reduce their capital expenditures on Painting by 10%, should I stop now?" Then I just shut up and waited. Bill then stated that they are planning on painting this year and that he wanted our information so we could be invited to the pre-bid meeting...

Here was a guy who told me never to call back. I did anyway but used the techniques from the Score Selling™ course, with no fluff at all and I got a positive result."
--Tripp Swift, Benise-Dowling National Painting

"I want to break CLIENT™ and LANC™ down to the basics and create a laminated card that will remind us of what to do prior to going into a customer session. I never understood my sales tactics before. I just picked things up and used them when they fit. This put everything into perspective."
--Stephen W., National Sales Manager, Industrial Sales

"The Sales Training from Score Selling™ has given me tangible means to sell more by planning better, getting more focus on the team's sales plans and better understanding of motivators to help sales staff achieve their goals."
--Bruce G., Automation Manager, Manufacturing Sales

I recently landed a major account and I can directly attribute my success to strategies learned from Score Selling™...
The prospect was an entertainment company in Los Angeles. I had attempted to reach them several times over the course of about a year. I didn't have a specific target in mind because I was not sure who the decision maker was. I left messages that were never returned. I had all but given up then I took Kevin's Score Selling™ course.
In the course I learned how to craft voice and email messages that were more likely to get a response. I was a bit skeptical but I tried it out. I learned how to obtain an email address using Kevin's training. Ultimately my communications conveyed a message that they would be doing themselves a disservice by not responding and learning more about the services that I had to offer. That message was forwarded to the Director of Accounting. After a couple of brief phone conversations, an "elevator pitch", and an email or two I found myself in Los Angeles meeting with the COO, CFO, Controller and Director of accounting.
Within a couple of weeks of that meeting the prospect became a new client and entered into an exclusive vendor contract with my company. I highly recommend Score Selling™ to anyone in sales. It is my experience that if you follow Kevin's program you will see a return on investment almost immediately.
--Jacob Robertson, Sales, Szabo Associates, Inc

"I am taking a more proactive goal in knowing my sales goal and striving to surpass it. It has allowed me to understand how to really listen to a customer needs.
--C. Nelson, Territory Sales

"Reinforces our practice of productivity (and efforts to increase), planning and time management. Helps understand not only the value to the company but to the individual sales reps. I have found the "group" training sessions very helpful ... specifically, the role-playing techniques in communicating with our clients and prospects and overcoming rebuttals etc. Out of the program I found the role playing techniques the most beneficial."
--Randy N., Sales Team Leader, Financial Industry

"I can attest my ability to sell more is a result of the Score Selling™, specifically because of the focus on applying these principles at the beginning of the sales process. It's a good program to refresh selling principles."
--Dennis M., Sales Specialist, Industrial Equipment Sales

"Kevin brought up so many ideas that never even crossed my mind! Great training! The questions I ask my customers!! I loved the idea of the poking questions that I can ask the customers in regards to quoting."
--S. Brown, Sales

"Score Selling™ Sales Training helps me by remembering what's in it for me as a result of making sales goals. And nudge the customer for more information so I can have a better understanding of situation."
-- Ben P., Electronic Automation Sales

"I took Kevin's Score Selling class over a period of many months and found him to be enthusiastic about his subject. Of particular benefit to me was the Score Selling's approach to time management and task tracking. I would recommend this to all."
--Andrew Parlour, Strategic Account Manager at Kliklok Woodman

"Score Selling™ Sales Training has equipped me to sell more by implementing the approach techniques and focus more time on key accounts which will allow for more success and opportunities."
--Brandon B., Large Motor Sales, Heavy Equipment

"I utilized the Score Selling™ sales training solution starting in June 2008 through to 2009 and again in 2010. I was part of an executive operations team at Landair responsible for implementing a sales training solution for our sales team. We selected Score Selling™ and, after administering a Sales Assessment, implemented the Score Selling™ Sales Training solution for our sales team. I found the program very effective in driving productive sales activities, specifically in the areas of prospecting, time management and lead generation. Kevin was also instrumental in building our sales process into the salesforce.com platform, ensuring conformity with the business needs of the operation and in training the sales team in it's use. I also called on Kevin's expertise to supplement my recruiting and hiring of new sales team members and in ramping up new sales trainees; he contributed significantly to the assembling of the company's new sales-hire training manual. I trust Kevin and his organization and highly recommend the Score Selling™ solution."
--Creighton Zirkle, Senior Transportation Manager at Pilot Travel Centers

"I try to insert more positive statements into conversations with customers. More confidence."
--JC, Corporate Sales

"I will be able to sell more as a result of the Score Selling™ Sales Training because I am following some steps of time management trying to organize better my day and I am going to ask the TAM to set a 15 minutes quote review as an ongoing practice with the customer."
--Charles S., Sales Team Leader, Industrial Equipment Sales

"Kevin was very perceptive on personality types & styles. I will be able to combat competitive companies with Proof Statements; and feel I will be able to PULL more information out of the customers. It has already improved my skills in drawing out more information & being able to pinpoint the actual issue."
--Laura B., Sales Representative

"MY GOALSETTING PROCEDURE IS ALOT MORE DEFINED!! THIS TAUGHT ME HOW TO PUT SPINS ON OPPORTUNITES THAT IN THE PAST MIGHT HAVE BEEN LOST."

--Larry M., Sales

"The Sales Training from Score Selling™ has given me tangible means to sell more by doing a better job at qualifying quotes and learning what questions to ask."
--Sharon L., Application Engineer, Industrial Sales

"I learned to not give up easily, to ask the question: Really, Why? or Why do you feel that way, and let the customer open up. And how to handle some common objections better."
--Ben S., Sales

"I sell more after being in Score Selling™ Sales Training because I started qualifying my requests and I am now more focused on the customer by understanding every customer's specific need or concern and then providing solutions even with experiencing hesitation on the customer's part."
--K. G., Sales Engineer, Industrial

"I take more ownership of what do. Dig deeper and add value... One key factor "Listen."
--C. W., Sales Representative

"Score Selling has been beneficial by giving me a different perspective when making sales calls. Since we are in field of limited prospects it is good to speak in a manner that promotes what the client wants verses what we want. It really has been helpful in the prospecting side of the business."
--Michael P., Sales Professional

"I attribute my ability to sell more as a result of the Score Selling™ training, specifically because it basically reminded me to ask more questions and it gives you other ideas to think through the process."
--Dale R., Large Motor Specialist, Manufacturing Sales

"The Score Selling™ training has given me the tools I need to be successful and the confidence that is needed when speaking with our clients. I was able to make my first sale after the class. Kevin taught in a way that it was not only fun but was easy to understand. He changed my way of thinking about sales. My personal opinion is that he is a great teacher. Would I recommend Score Selling™? Yes, for students like myself who have never had any sales

experience he opened doors about selling that had previously scared me to death and took the fear out of what I thought would be really hard; he made selling easy and gave the tools to overcome all of the objections that we face when speaking with prospects."
--I. Kendrick, Sales, Recovery Services Industry

"I ask more questions of the customer in order to help get the sale. I am asking more questions now."
--SB, Sales

"Score Selling™ helps me to sell more by understanding the customers requirement and to show the customer how committed you are to help their specific application."
--MN, Application Engineer, Manufacturing Sales

"I learned new ideas on how to communicate with the customers. I will be researching the competition a little more to find out where we stand. To find out if our pricing is too high or quality is an issue with the customer and offer accessories with each sale if possible."
--VN, Territory Sales

"Score Selling™ Sales Training equips me to sell more by trying to qualify projects more both before and after quoting."
--William R., Senior Application Engineer, Industrial Equipment Sales

"Kevin's training was very practical and based on usable techniques. I will pay even more attention to asking open ended questions and gauging my customer's real concerns. The training helped solidify ideas offered in our own training. We were able to practice real techniques and the exercises helped reinforce the theory."
--M. Moss, Territory Sales

"I can directly attribute my ability to sell more as a result of Score Selling™, specifically because I am using the training to refine my sales approach considering the CLIENT™ and LANC™ tools. Some of the approaches learned from the training have shaved rough edges off of my sales acumen and will enable me to provide better customer service and encourage a sale while leaving less "icky salesperson residue."

--Jason K., Sales, MFG

"I will be able to sell more as a result of the Score Selling™ Sales Training because I use better techniques for listening & asking questions and now have improved techniques of selling."
--Paul M., Controls Sales Engineer, MFG

"I learned to use my personal time to increase my knowledge about our products. Sharing familiarities with other salespeople and working together as a team was a great way to learn new information as well as expand current knowledge."
--KO, Sales Support

"The Sales Training from Score Selling™ has given me tangible means to sell more by helping me to focus more on trying to put the pieces of the project together in order to best understand the whole of the situation, increase the quality of my quote, and increase the quality and effectiveness of my direct customer contacts."
--Brandon M., Sales Engineer, MFG

"I learned techniques to counter some customer issues re: price/quality, etc. and ways to offer customer "fries" with the motors."
--CK, Corporate Sales

"Score Selling™ has helped me with increasing the effectiveness of the voice mails that I leave for clients. As sometimes it is hard to reach a client (or potential client) on the phone, a well-planned voice mail that leaves them with a reason to want to call you back increases our chances of gaining business. I would recommend this training course to others. It has provided me with new ways to not only reach out to the clients but also innovative ways in which to overcome the objections that we encounter when asking for the client's business."
--John Shearer, Account Manager, Commercial Recovery Industry

"I can sell more after being in Score Selling™ Sales Training because I spend more up front time qualifying CLIENTS and focus on true potential instead of hopeful accounts."

--Michael U., Automation Sales Engineer, Electronic Automation Sales

"I look forward to try out some of the objection handling techniques. Improve communication with the customer."
--RT, Territory Sales

"I can attribute my ability to sell more due to Score Selling™ sales training, specifically because of Time Management and Qualifying leads and customers better and Ideas of how to manage my time and questions to ask when prospecting a customer or project."
--Marc M., Southeast Large Machines Sales, Heavy Equipment

"His ability to make us think about what we are doing was very refreshing. It encouraged the salespeople to continue to question the customers on Why us". With the notes that I took and the suggestions from some of the previous groups, I will be able to have more "ammo" on selling of the products and services that we have to offer. I think that this will also enable the sales's groups to communicate better between each other."
--Krista S., Sales Leader

"Score Selling™ helps me to sell more by qualifying the lead better on the front side and reviewing your own processes and how you do your job."
--James S., Large Motor Specialist, Heavy Equipment Sales

"I learned to set another goal for myself as well as handling objections using turn key sample. It has given me new ideas on how to strategize better and put us on the top of customer's vendor list."
--PG, Territory Sales

"Score Selling™ Sales Training equips me to sell more by giving me a better focus on improving communications with every element and it's always good to re-evaluate how you go through the sales process and see where you can take better ownership of areas that can lead to losing the order."
--Ken S., Application Engineer, Industrial Equipment Sales

"Kevin was very personable and likeable. Now I focus more on the strengths we have as a negotiating tool. I am more confident in handling objections."
--Clay W., Sales Leader

"I will be able to sell more as a result of the Score Selling™ Sales Training because I ask more questions when trying to close a sale and use fresh techniques for obtaining information."
--Terri W., Sales Supervisor - Automation, Electronic Automation Sales

"I think Kevin's training is VERY beneficial to handling the types of customers I have. I am going to put the training I have received into practice in my everyday job. Primarily by handling objections by having the customer explain their true needs."
--K. Jones, Sales

"The Sales Training from Score Selling™ has given me tangible means to sell more by - Follow up, listening for unidirectional cues from the customer and being better prepared to get the customer to spill the beans. I think I'll utilize the 15-minute meeting follow up for some key opportunities and it has enhanced my skills and mindset about getting key information from customers."
--Orlando C., Sales Engineer, Industrial Equipment Sales

"I believe this would be essential to future sale opportunities and this would also keep everyone in sync which would avoid confusion of any sort. I will try to find more ways to assist our sales-Reps in which could make a difference in Sales. It helped build a strong level of confidence in knowing what the company has to offer despite the challenges customers may pose in comparison to our competitors."
--MS, Sales Support

"I can sell more after being in Score Selling™ Sales Training because I will start to use the CLIENT process and I can spend more time on what is important and less time on busy work."
--Robert M., Sales, MFG

ScoreSelling™

The Game of Selling More

By Kevin Leveille

President

Score Selling, LLC

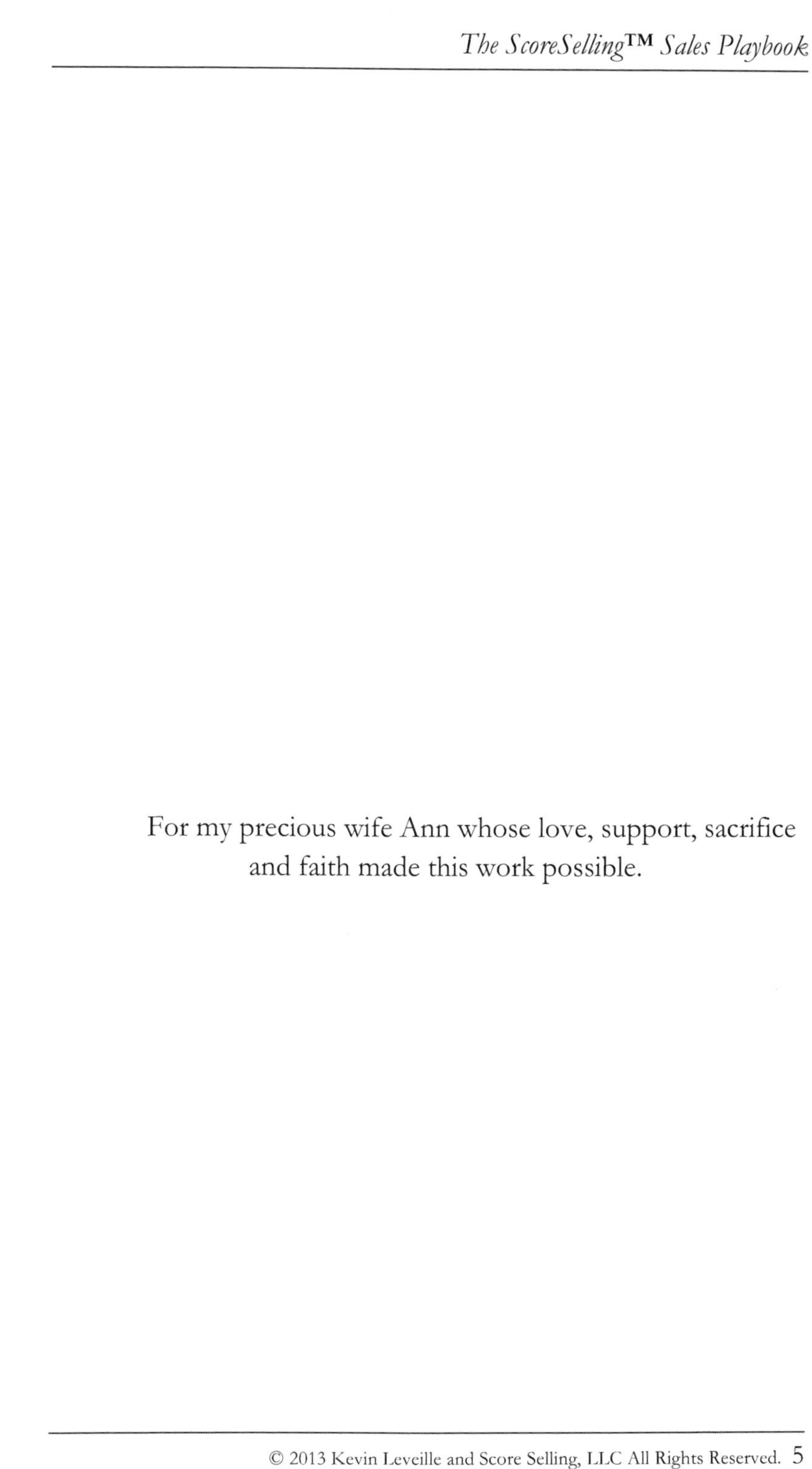

For my precious wife Ann whose love, support, sacrifice and faith made this work possible.

Disclaimer of Warranty. Nothing in this book constitutes or implies in any way any warranty as to results obtained from the use of the information herein. All use of the principles and information of this book are at the sole risk of you, the Reader. In no event shall Author be liable for any direct or indirect, special, punitive, incidental or consequential damages for any reason based on any act or omission of Reader related directly or indirectly to any information or training provided by Author for which Reader, or its agents, employees or contractors use, employ or follow in their Business. Further, Author makes no warranty concerning the accuracy of any information given over the telephone, by its employees, thru web-site access or any informational product. Author does not guarantee, warranty or represent that Reader shall increase any Business, sales, income or performance income, and Author shall not be liable to Reader for any or all monetary losses at any time whether resulting from job loss, income loss, or customer loss. Reader acknowledges and agrees that selling is a volatile business and that Author cannot guarantee Reader any increase in sales or income.

Contents

Part I: Welcome

Chapter 1: **Introduction**

Welcome to ScoreSelling™!

This book will take you through the ScoreSelling™ 3.0 Professional Sales program.

ScoreSelling™ 3.0 in a nutshell

Sales success comes from persistent hard work applied in a smart way on a consistent basis. ScoreSelling™ is a sales solution designed to help a salesperson apply maximum effort, intelligence and consistency to win the game of sales. Whatever your experience level in sales, ScoreSelling™ 3.0 will help you sell more and faster than ever before possible.

What's in this Book

Selling begins with goal setting. That's where ScoreSelling™ begins as well. We will step you through the essentials of goal setting and time management.

We will develop and refine your message and re-purpose that message for use in multiple ways and mediums from in-person conversations to phone to email to letters. Presentation development will also be addressed.

We will treat prospecting in depth and as you have never seen it before. You will learn ways to turn obstacles such as voicemail into an asset for delivering your message and deal with even the most resistant prospect. You will learn to use information-age concepts such as streaming to deliver your message in manners that can open lots of doors.

We will discuss Objection Handling with LANC™ that will show how truly simple it is for you to engage your prospects in meaningful dialogue.

We will address in-depth sales qualification. You will learn methods and approaches that will completely redefine your concept of qualification and you will learn how to use what were previously unapproachable conversation pieces to allow your prospect to open up and tell you what you need to know.

The final section of the book will deal in great detail with sales process and how it all comes together. You will explore new ways to structure your in-person meetings and interactions with the prospect and will dramatically improve your ability to carry sales cycles through to successful conclusion.

Again, welcome to ScoreSelling™ 3.0!

Chapter 2: **The Heartache of Sales**

Selling is not an easy profession; it's a difficult one. A very difficult one, loaded with obstacles and challenges which stand in the way of getting the deal done or enough deals done, to make it worth your while to keep on going with it as a career. While not everyone who enters the sales profession will get to experience success, everyone who enters the sales profession will at one point in time certainly get to experience the heartache of sales.

Heartache might be the moment that you are fully confronted with the fact that prospects—people—do not always do what you expect them to. Or it might be that you lose that big deal you were counting on and you're not sure why. Maybe you've heard someone describe what a salesperson is, or maybe you've even met someone you think is the epitome of a great salesperson and you felt that you could never be like them.

Maybe it was the lousy way a prospect spoke to you when you called, the one that made you want to bang your head on your desk. Maybe it was just going home to your spouse and having to relate (again) what was not yet possible for you to afford. Perhaps it was showing up at another family function or friendly gathering and wondered why everyone else seemed so successful and happy with what they did for a living while you—well, you still were not.

The heartache of sales is what drives salespeople out of the business faster and more certainly than any other thing. Heartache quickly takes down someone in between jobs who comes to "try out" the sales profession. But it also can take out those who *are* cut out for the profession, who *do* have what it takes, but who get too big a streak of heartache before they ever get to taste the successful stuff that keeps salespeople in the business of selling for life.

Uncertainty Causes Heartache

The one thing that must be significantly reduced or eliminated from all aspects of your sales life is uncertainty, because uncertainty is the main cause of heartache. Uncertainty causes far more stress and heartache than the loss of the deal itself. It's not the slap of rejection that hurts the most; it's the shock of the slap. And the repercussions of going forward living in fear, trying to avoid getting slapped again. Many people say that is just the life of the salesperson.

It is not.

Reducing uncertainty means that you reduce the amount of time you spend with someone who is probably not going to buy from you. It means ceasing to churn and worry, because you have the information about what is going to happen, you are not waiting to see what does happen. If you feel that is a tall order, you are correct. It is a tall order to claim that it is possible to be put into a position of power, to have the information you need to go about your sales day in confident expectation of good results.

But that is exactly what ScoreSelling™ 3.0 will do for you.

Chapter 3: **Scoring**

That which is measured can be improved; that which is not measured cannot be improved.

What Scoring Does for You

Scoring is essential to success. It gives you the ability to reflect the value of your sales activities today, rather than waiting 90 days for the orders to come in.

Would you watch the Super Bowl if you had to wait 90 days for the score?

In the same way, ScoreSelling™ 3.0 captures the future value of your sales activities and represents it to you as you perform those activities today.

Where There's Smoke There's Fire

Quality sales activities leave a signature behind them. ScoreSelling™ 3.0 creates a situation that enables you to *see* that signature and assign a score to it.

Traditional means of recording sales activities (# calls, # meetings, # proposals, etc.) have some value, but are limited.

Take meetings for example. Meeting types differ widely amongst salespeople; some salespeople get a lot accomplished in their meetings and others do not. A truly effective score would reflect the difference, which ScoreSelling™ 3.0 does.

Do not try to absorb all of this right now. You will need time to test it to see it yourself; this is the reason ScoreSelling™ 3.0 has a training program, to allow you the time and opportunity to see it working for you. Just keep an open mind and you will be amazed with what happens.

Recording

Recording is essential to scoring, of course, since you cannot report a score you do not record. At first, you will notice that you will be recording more than you are used to but the tremendous benefits you receive as a result of this minor administrative task will more than compensate for any initial inconvenience.

Record Everything

Record everything. In golf you record every stroke. In every major professional sport every statistic is captured for analysis. They do that for the same reason you will do that—to improve. That which can be measured can be improved—that which is not measured cannot be improved.

What will come to you as a result of this exercise is visibility. Once that cloud of uncertainty is removed you will see things you never did before; things you need to stop doing and things you need to do more of. At that point, as a success minded salesperson, you will be sold on the tremendous benefits that come from record keeping in ScoreSelling™ 3.0.

	Week 1	Week 2	Week 3	Week 4	Total Points	Total Revenue
Jim	1,700	2,200	2,100	2,300	8,300	$ 250,000

Sally	1,600	1,700	1,900	1,700	6,900	$ 140,000
Tom	600	700	800	700	2,700	$ 35,000

In the table above, three salespeople's scores are reported by week.

- Jim knows that keeping his score high leads to the revenue he wants.
- Sally knows this as well; she just needs some help and training to get her scores higher.
- Tom just doesn't care.

Toolsets

In ScoreSelling™ 3.0 you will be recording *every relevant* sales activity you undertake. Some salespeople choke on that stipulation, so if that's you here's some good news; you will not need to fill out reams of paper with useless facts. You simply need to use the toolsets provided; learn them in the training and apply them in the field.

ScoreSelling™ 3.0 toolsets give you the ability to plan well, execute and record results in special toolsets designed specifically for the salesperson. The toolsets link up to allow you to manage your sales prospects and sales cycles fluidly. The score that will represent your success is calculated within these toolsets.

Implications of the Score

Scoring provides visibility to what the true FUTURE value of your sales activities are TODAY. It keeps your attention where it belongs; on contributing enough high quality sales activity to close the sales volume you want.

The score shows without a doubt that by increasing the quantity and quality of your sales activities you can fully expect to close the type of sales you want.

Over time, you will see your weekly score rise and fall. When it rises you know you are well on your way to achieving sales success as represented by higher revenue and income. While you should not experience the results of higher revenue and higher income immediately, you can rest assured that you soon will.

Scoring automatically increases the value of your activities because you as a competitive salesperson will want to increase the points you are scoring.

Scoring In Summary

You can see that the way to score big on a weekly basis is to see a lot of prospects and to get them qualified. However, you will also find that the additional points you get from prospecting and from good time management will add up as well.

Again, do not get caught up trying to absorb or reject this information upfront. You will be covering this in more detail throughout this course.

Part II: Goals & Time

Chapter 4: About Goals

Goal setting is essential to sales performance. In this chapter you are going to look at what goals are, what they are not and how to use them to your advantage.

What are Goals?

Goals are a desired result that must occur before a certain date. For example, a goal might be stated as follows;

"I will close 100% of my quota within nine months of the start of the year, or by September 30."

Or

"I will sell $1,200,000 in new business in the third quarter of this year."

Or,

"My annual profit margin target is 35%, an increase of 10% over last year."

Four Reasons Why You Should Set Goals

First, you need to know where you are trying to get.

Second, on any given day you need to be able to discern if the actions you are taking are going to get you to your goals. All your activity flows backwards from the goal you set. Should I make calls today or go to the coffee shop with the guys? Should I go out to that industrial park and cold call or stay in the hotel and snack on YouTube? Should I make one more contact today or layoff early and go home? The answers to these questions are different for someone who is able to reference a goal they have set versus for someone who has no goals at all.

Third, you want to be in conscious control of your own professional future. Without setting goals the salesperson puts himself at the disposal of someone else who has in fact set goals. For many salespeople, the goals for their career are set solely by their boss. You do not want this. Set your own goals.

And finally, considering your own goals will help you determine if you and the prospect should continue investing time in the sales process together. The prospect usually has very specific goals he is trying to accomplish. As far as you are concerned he may be more interested in grabbing a quick competitive quote to justify his first choice. Or maybe he does not want to pay as much as your solution is worth. Whatever it is, you as a salesperson need to be able to discern if the prospect's goals and your goals are the same. Having set clear goals for yourself will allow you to answer such an important question.

Three Problems with Goals

The first problem with goals is that most people do not have them at all. The majority of those who do have goals have not taken the time to write them down. That means they have not taken the important step of really defining the goal.

The second problem with goal setting is that the goal is not reasonable or based in any reality. The goal target is set way too high; maybe the salesperson's goal is to become the top producer of all time in twelve months. Rarely is this the motivational force it is presumed to be, only becoming an excuse for the salesperson to feel like a failure and give up way too soon, as soon as it becomes clear that the goal is unlikely to be reached.

The third problem has to do with what happens once the goal is articulated. It ends up on the shelf, where it can do absolutely no good at all since the goal is kept safe and sound in the document binder where it was conceived, never to be referenced again. The next time the goal is read is when the office is being cleaned out (or the salesperson is changing jobs.)

Putting Goal Setting to Work for You

Goal setting that does some good for you is goal setting that takes place as a deliberate, specific exercise and which concludes with a document which can be easily referenced on an ongoing basis and against which progress can be verified.

A deliberate exercise means that you take the time to define a specific result in a definite period of time. Set a reasonable goal that has some basis in reality, either from your own personal experience or from that of an experienced salesperson that is helping you to define your goals.

A reference-able document means if you want to sell $2,000,000 in new business this year, it does little good to set the goal in January and not reference it again until December. Rather, make use of that goal and plan out an action strategy for achieving the goal. For instance, you would take the $2,000,000 goal and break it into four quarters of $500,000 each. Further, you may find it helpful to break the quarterly target down into three months of $167,000 each. You would then reference that goal on a weekly or a daily basis and measure your progress against it.

Finally, you would make estimates of the types of pre-sales activities you would need to engage which would reasonably conclude in the sales result described in your target goal. For instance if you have a five stage sales process (from first meeting to close) you would take into account the average amount of time spent at each stage and build a model which would allow you to measure whether you are doing enough of the right activities on a daily basis to keep you on target. So if your close ratio from the last meeting is 50% where half of the prospects you have a closing meeting with become your customer and the average sale is $50,000, then you had better plan on getting 20 closing meetings this quarter, right?

Look at it again; what is your quarterly goal? $500,000; correct? What is your average sale? $50,000; right? How many sales to get to the quarterly goal? 10; where 10 x $50,000 = $500,000. How many closing meetings do you need to hold to be reasonably sure of getting those 10 sales of $50,000 each? Well, your close ratio is half, or 50%, right? So then, if you had only 10 meetings, you could expect 5 sales to close; taking 5 x the average sale of $50,000 is $250,000; which leaves you only halfway there. So, you'd better double the number of closing meetings you expect to have this quarter from 10 to 20. Now, when you apply your closing ratio of 50% you end up with half of 20 or 10 total sales. Multiply that times your average sale of $50,000 gets you to $500,000.

What is now possible is to manage the upstream sales activities that need to take place and to track your effectiveness on a daily and weekly basis. In this way, it is possible to track sales activities right back to the average number of first meetings--and even before that to the average number of phone calls--which need to be done to get the closing meetings you need to get the number of sales you need to hit your target.

Presto! Just watch the chronic feelings of uncertainty in sales get cut down to size! Setting up goals in this way means rejection has nowhere near the level of effect on your success, since you already know how many you have to win, and how to structure your pre-sales activities to ensure you end up with the result you want to get.

Setting Goals Using PROVEN™

The PROVEN™ Vision Management system is a good way to go about articulating the reasons behind your goal. One of the common problems with setting goals is that even a reasonable goal can seem daunting once it is defined. PROVEN™ is a simple method designed to make the goal setting exercise fluid, even fun.

There are six steps in the PROVEN™ process;

1. Privilege: establish a list of those things for which you are grateful. Feel free to include things like health, family, friends, job, and etc.
2. Relief: now make a list of those things you would like to be free of. Include debt, low income, etc.

3. Opportunity: now you are ready to begin describing the goals of what you want and by when.
4. VIPs: describe the key people in your life. Who are they and what will their reaction be as they witness your achievements?
5. Experience: find a way to begin experiencing the results now. No longer see cold calling, for instance, as a thankless chore, but one that is directly responsible for leading you to the results you want.
6. Normalize: make viewing and reviewing your goals a consistent part of your schedule, at least once per week if not more.

By using PROVEN™ you will rapidly bring reality and color to your goals.

Chapter 5: **Setting Goals and a Plan to Achieve Them**

Goal setting requires an understanding of where you've been before you can begin to gauge where you want to be.

Last Quarter Review

Baseline Your Top Sales Transactions

Describe your last quarter performance in detail. List the accounts that purchased your solutions and the revenue associated with those transactions. List as many actually happened. If more than 25, list the top 25; decide for yourself whether it makes sense to continue beyond the first 25.

What is your honest impression of this exercise? Did you discover anything in doing it? How strong a grasp do you have on the types and volume of business currently being done in your territory? Top sales professionals and those on their way to the top know this information very well.

Describe Your Sales Process

A sales process is a sequence of events. ALWAYS. It is never a series of haphazard events. In conversation almost every professional salesperson claims to have a process that they sell by. In practice, they may, but they often have trouble articulating it. In those cases, the reality is simply that no real process exists. The reason is often that the salesperson fears a process that may bind the prospect or make them uncomfortable. This is a valid fear.

What are the steps and stages of your sales process?

Many salespeople have no pre-defined process; do you? List the steps and stages of your sales process that you used to bring in the revenue for last quarter. What are the key stages? Think of sequence—what can never happen unless another step happens first? Example: you cannot deliver a proposal before you ______. That's an example of process.

What did you do first with a prospect?

What did you do in your first meetings with prospects? Did you have an agenda or did you just show up and see how things developed? What were the deliverables to the prospect? What did you demand in return? What is an example of a great first meeting you had? Why?

How did you determine they were a good prospect?

What were your good prospects? What was an example of someone you could not wait to get in front of? Why? Did they buy?

When did you offer a proposal & what did they need to show you to warrant your time in preparing a proposal?

Under what conditions were you ready to offer a proposal to a prospect? What did they need to do first? Why? Did they simply have to request pricing? What were some pre-conditions you demanded which, if they were not there, you were not going to issue a proposal?

What came after the proposal?

After the proposal what happened? Did you fall back and wait? What was the customer tasked with doing? Why? When you gave a proposal, were you merely hoping to get back in the door for a closing meeting or did you know you would be back? How often were you right?

What was the last thing you did prior to booking the order as revenue?

Describe your closing process. What was the very last thing you did prior to closing the order? Was it always the same? Why?

Close Ratios

Close ratios are traditionally the rate at which you close business when measured from some earlier point in the sales process. Some sales organizations track the close ratios from early on in the sales process, even back to the first meeting. In that instance, a salesperson that saw 20 new first meetings and closed 2 sales from them would be said to have a close ratio of 10%.

For your purposes you will be going much more granular than that. You will be tracking close ratios on a stage-to-stage basis. This means that you will be tracking the success rate of converting from, for instance, the first meeting to the second meeting. Stated another way, what percent of first meetings translated to second meetings?

Why track this? This is tracked because it shows the value of what is being presented or discussed in one stage insofar as the prospect is interested enough to invite you back. How effective is the information the salesperson is presenting? How impressed is the customer by this information? Is this impression sufficient that the customer invites you back or opts to take another step in the process—and towards the sale—with you and your company?

This is important information. By tracking the effectiveness of your conversion from one stage to the next, you will begin to spot hidden trends. Salespeople who are ineffective at converting a prospect efficiently from the first meeting to the second meeting stage of the process may learn from other salespeople who are effective in this stage. Information about who and what is effective can in this way be leveraged throughout the sales organization to close more business without increasing activity, but rather improving the quality of it.

Problems with Close Ratios

Often, salespeople struggle with this exercise; that's understandable. But sometimes salespeople attempt to claim this exercise does not apply to them. Each prospect is so different from one to the next, they claim, that to attempt to typify any type of ratio is pointless. But the fact remains that close ratios are not figments of imagination, they are points of fact. You make a certain number of calls or have a certain number of first meetings—that's fact. As a result you have a certain number of sales—also a fact. The ratio between these two numbers is not conjecture or wishful thinking; it is a matter of simple fact. Tracking these and other numbers is the start of controlling them.

Your Close Ratios

Based on your last quarter, what were your conversion rates from stage to stage of your sales process? How effective were you at each stage? Do you have this information? If not, you can estimate it by looking at your planner, listing those meetings that were at each stage of your sales process and do the numbers.

It is important to understand how you arrived at the results you achieved last quarter. Understanding these numbers will give you an objective target to begin working on improving those numbers. We will spend more time on this in subsequent chapters.

Summary

This may have been a painful exercise for you, it is for most. Some even get so frustrated they try to skip it; but its impractical, since so much of what you will be doing next depends upon it.

Again, the reason we are delving so deeply into your defined sales process is to ensure you have a firm grasp of what is going on in your market and can take the additional steps with the ScoreSelling™ System to improve upon it.

Goals

You have an understanding of what you have done and what you can do. Now you are equipped to lay out your goals for the coming year.

Your Goals This Year

Describe your goals this year. Consider items such as revenue, profit, personal income or commissions.

Who or What says you have to do that?

For example, is there a Company quota or incentive plan? Are these your own personal goals?

Are these goals REASONABLE?

Why or why not? Have you accomplished this or something similar before? Has anyone? Reasonability in goal setting is essential to the believability of the goal.

As an extreme example consider someone with an average sale of $1,000 who sets a goal of selling $10,000,000. Anything is possible, but not everything is reasonable, as this individual will soon find when they attempt to define the sales activities they will need to employ to get to that goal.

Has anything changed to prohibit, enhance or affect these goals?

For instance, the economy, the time of year, etc. Are there any adjustments that need to be made?

Quarterly Goals

What do you want to get accomplished this quarter?

Sales Activities

You have defined what results you want this year; now you take the vital step of defining how it will happen.

You took a swing at defining your sales process and the conversion rates and types earlier.

Moving forward, you will be using that framework to forecast the types of activities you need to take to accomplish your goal.

What is your average transaction size? Divide your total revenue by the total number of transactions.

Ex. $2,000,000 / 10 transactions = $200,000

Based on your Average Transaction size, how many transactions will you need to get this year to achieve your total revenue goal?

Ex. Goal of $3,000,000 divided by Ave Transaction of $200,000 = 15 new transactions

How many closing interviews do you need to get those 20 new sales? 50% close rate at the late stage is typical.

Ex. Since only 50% of your closing meetings end in a sale, you need two good closing meetings for every one sale. Therefore, if you need a total of 15 new transactions, you need 30 good closing meetings

How many proposal meetings do you need to bring about a closing meeting?

Ex. You need 3 proposal meetings for every closing meeting, so you need 90 proposals (3 x 30 = 90.)

How many needs analysis meetings to get one proposal meeting?

Ex. You need 2 analysis meetings for every proposal you do, so you need 180 analysis meetings (2 x 90 = 180)

How many introductory meetings to get one needs analysis meeting?

Ex. You need 2 introductory meetings to get one analysis meeting so you need 360 analysis meetings (2 x 180 = 360)

How many prospecting calls to get one introductory meeting?

Ex. It takes about 10 calls to get one good introductory meeting so you need 3,600 calls (10 x 360 = 3,600)

Your Average Work Week

Once you have completed this exercise you will be able to extract a snapshot average workweek. This is a week which contains the average number of each type of meeting which you will be holding on your way to reaching your goal. You can additionally estimate the hours needed for these activities. Again, for experienced users, you can and should estimate point projections.

Summary

Congratulations! You have taken the steps to success which 99.9% of salespeople never take. Get ready to see some great things flow out of this exercise and into your business.

Target Accounts

In this section you will be assembling a list of accounts and opportunities that you will use to get you to goal.

Building the List

Building your Target Account list is a process of refinement rather than one of perfection. There are four sections you will be tapping to layout a foundation for your list.

Customers

The first place you look for a likely prospect is in those accounts that have already bought your solution. They have the faith in your company and in you if you were the one who originally sold it to them. So here is where you can look for some low hanging fruit.

List a few customer names that you believe may have some potential for doing business with you again over the next year. List why you feel there is some potential there, how much approximately and any other comments.

Do not be over concerned with nailing down every detail. That is not the point here. The point here is to brainstorm a few accounts that can form a basis for reaching your goals this year.

Industries

With the industries section you are changing tack and beginning to think about acquiring business from new prospects over the course of the year. Take a few industries where you feel there may be some potential this year. Think in terms of those industries where you already have customers. This will make referencing easier. Ultimately similar companies in the same industry tend to have similar problem sets that will help immensely in qualifying the account.

Again, list those industries where you think there might be some potential. Next to each industry, list as many accounts as you can think of in that industry. Again, you are merely looking to lay a foundation for more detail later.

Referrals

Referrals are contacts you have which may be able to point you towards some prospects for your solution. These can be from any walk of your life, but most business solutions tend to find their best sources of referrals from their current customers. If that's the case for you, realize this is still a separate exercise from the one you did two steps ago in compiling customers you will be pursuing for business this year. In that step you were thinking of potential customers who could buy again. In this step you will be looking at customers you have which will possibly provide references or referrals to other prospective accounts or customers.

After you have listed the customer names, layout a few accounts that you have reason to suspect may be able to refer you to (if there are any you can think of.)

Finally, list anyone else who might be worth a phone call or cup of coffee to determine if they might be able to provide you a referral or two. No shooting in the dark here, though—this step is about listing credible sources of possible referrals, not listing everyone you know willy-nilly to interrogate for leads.

Raw Prospect List

This list is about what may be anything from the finishing touches on your considerable Target Account List, or the means by which you will be finding 80% or more of your Target Accounts.

List those databases you know of and have access to which can be a source of a list of Target Accounts. Think in terms of D&B, salesgenie.com, onesource.com, etc. You may have industry specific databases that are often better refined for your type of prospect. All the better.

List these sources and any comments about how best to use them, or what needs to take place in order for you to use them—do you need to get permission, or even just do the preliminary research to see if you should use them?

Once you have completed this initial brainstorm, you are ready for the next section.

Annual Target Opportunities

The second step in the list of Target Accounts refinement process is the Annual Target Opportunity list. As already stated, the process of selecting your Target Accounts is one of refinement not perfection. What you see in this next section is a list to describe who your Annual Target Accounts should be.

This section requires more commitment from you, more professional deliberation. This part of the exercise is not meant to be done in one sitting, but added to and refined over a period of time. However, you should aim to have it completed certainly before the end of the first quarter of the applicable year.

For now, look back to the lists you have generated and add any account you see there which meet the requirements describing an Annual Target Opportunity. If you have more than the 25 listed, you can either add more pages, or just go with the 25.

Be sure, however, that you are adding names credibly and professionally, not names for the sake of adding names. This part of the exercise is about adding names that fit the specific requirements for an Annual Target Opportunity. That means that this list should be added to in a manner consistent with a professional who intends to conduct at least an initial sales campaign with these accounts.

Seeing the list implode into a pile of "Dead" prospects a few weeks into the sales cycle would tend to suggest that not enough knowledge of the accounts was used to compile the list in the first place. If you can add only one name here, but can do it credibly, that is fine—you will be building it out later anyway.

Forecast Quarterly Target Opportunities

The final step of the Target Account List refinement process comes now; Forecast Quarterly Target Opportunities.

Additional detail is required for the accounts here. This may begin to resemble something like the forecast that your company has you fill out each month or quarter. List the accounts that you have reason to believe are closeable this quarter. Then list the reasons they are closeable this quarter.

"Most Likely" is a designation that refers to the volume of revenue or business that is highly probable. "Best Case" is that extra business which could close if the very best circumstances occur.

Conclusion

Great job! You have now taken the important step of laying the foundation for achieving the goals you have set for yourself.

Chapter 6: Time Management

What is Time Management for Salespeople?

The discipline of reducing your day to the most basic common denominator of hours and minutes and measuring how much good you can do with those hours and minutes.

Why Time Management is Important

You need to stay focused doing what makes you and your company money; selling.

A good time management system provides another data point for how well you are doing.

A good time management system tells you the truth about what is happening with your time.

90% of Salespeople are Working at Less Than 20% Effectiveness

It is not that salespeople are unplugging for 80% of their day--though to be sure, some are—but more that the combination of low work levels combine with the increasing challenges facing salespeople on a daily basis to reduce their productivity in a kind of vicious cycle over time.

The volume of self-made millionaires is not a testament to luck, but to hard work, discipline and smarts applied now. Keeping activated and productive means you must have a way of getting a hold of the passing of time and putting it to work for you.

Failing to get a good hold on time means you could experience a consistent sense of being behind, of accumulating debt rather than wealth and of being generally dissatisfied with your professional career.

What Time Management Is Not

Time Management is not a natural ability. You may know of people you see as effective time managers—those type "A" individuals (I've got a theory of what that "A" stands for.) They are always in motion, charging around, "getting it done." They seem to be naturals and you might decide that if that is what it takes to be an effective time manager, then you will never be one.

But there is nothing about Time Management that is naturally occurring in a normal, well-adjusted human being. So don't sweat it if you found out that you don't have good Time Management skills.

What Time Costs

Did you ever take a minute to figure out what your time is worth? If you earn or want to earn $100,000 per year, for example, your hourly time is valued at the income divided by the hours in that year.

Working a 40 hour workweek x 50 weeks = 2,000 hours.

Income of $100,000 / 2,000 hours = $50.00 per hour.

The key to earning an income is to ensure that each hour you work is worth at least that amount. When you worked through the Goal setting exercise and got a baseline you were doing this.

What Time Saves

Effective time management is an incredibly powerful tool in getting you to your goals. Look below and see for yourself; numbers don't lie.

Income level is listed on the far left, with an hourly rate next to it. The value of finding an additional hour each day is listed from left to right for that income level.

Your Stats		Annual Gain from Finding Additional				
Income	Hourly	1 Hr	1.5 Hrs	2 Hrs	3 Hrs	4 Hrs
$ 25,000	$ 12.50	$ 3,125	$ 4,688	$ 6,250	$ 9,375	$ 12,500
$ 30,000	$ 15.00	$ 3,750	$ 5,625	$ 7,500	$ 11,250	$ 15,000
$ 35,000	$ 17.50	$ 4,375	$ 6,563	$ 8,750	$ 13,125	$ 17,500
$ 40,000	$ 20.00	$ 5,000	$ 7,500	$ 10,000	$ 15,000	$ 20,000
$ 50,000	$ 25.00	$ 6,250	$ 9,375	$ 12,500	$ 18,750	$ 25,000
$ 60,000	$ 30.00	$ 7,500	$ 11,250	$ 15,000	$ 22,500	$ 30,000
$ 75,000	$ 37.50	$ 9,375	$ 14,063	$ 18,750	$ 28,125	$ 37,500
$ 90,000	$ 45.00	$ 11,250	$ 16,875	$ 22,500	$ 33,750	$ 45,000
$ 100,000	$ 50.00	$ 12,500	$ 18,750	$ 25,000	$ 37,500	$ 50,000
$ 150,000	$ 75.00	$ 18,750	$ 28,125	$ 37,500	$ 56,250	$ 75,000
$ 200,000	$100.00	$ 25,000	$ 37,500	$ 50,000	$ 75,000	$100,000
$ 250,000	$125.00	$ 31,250	$ 46,875	$ 62,500	$ 93,750	$125,000
$ 300,000	$150.00	$ 37,500	$ 56,250	$ 75,000	$112,500	$150,000
$ 350,000	$175.00	$ 43,750	$ 65,625	$ 87,500	$131,250	$175,000
$ 400,000	$200.00	$ 50,000	$ 75,000	$100,000	$150,000	$200,000
$ 450,000	$225.00	$ 56,250	$ 84,375	$112,500	$168,750	$225,000
$ 500,000	$250.00	$ 62,500	$ 93,750	$125,000	$187,500	$250,000
			Time Gained			
	In Workweeks	6	9	13	19	25
	In Days Off	31	47	63	94	125

You can see that if you earn $100,000 (or want to) your hourly value is $50.00 per hour as we have already seen in the exercise above. But look at what happens to the value of your year when you can find an additional one-hour of value and put that to work for you on a daily basis. You can grow your overall income by $12,500 per year!

The good news is that this chart is not static—it is only an estimate to get you thinking. And that means you don't have to actually work for that hour—you can just get smarter or more effective in what you are doing with the hours you are already working.

So you could become a more effective prospector; a better presenter; a sharper closer. You could make more calls, see more people, and see more of the right people. You could get better with objection handling, better at qualifying, better at keeping a sales process together. You could be more effective in basic productive capabilities like time management and ensure you are up on time, out the door on time, in the field on time. You could use your cell phone more, listen to music less. You could stay a little later; work a little longer, there are a lot of areas you could hit to improve your overall experience of success.

And what if you could add more than one hour per day?

Time Debtor

Time debt is something that gets accumulated easier than credit card debt. Time debt comes when you commit to doing something and allocate insufficient time to complete it. Committing to be somewhere by a certain time when you know that a prior commitment keeps you too far away is one example. Promising to play with your kids when you finish working and then never finishing working is another (ouch) one. Time is simply too "free" to be accounted for so it is spent as a cheap resource, as if it is readily replenished, like a government handout.

But the day comes when the resource of time becomes too precious to buy with any amount of money. You will be better prepared for that moment if you learn to appreciate the true value of time sooner rather than later.

Ask yourself a few questions;

- Do you make too many commitments?
- When someone 'pops-in' do you drop everything to accommodate him or her?
- When a meeting is running out of control, do you know how to end it diplomatically?
- Do you work as work comes, or do you plan your workday to suit your life?

What if You Were On Trial?

What if you were on trial for the crime of being an excellent time-manager? That is, what if your time management skills were so renowned, the district attorney decided to prosecute you for them?

- Would there be enough evidence to convict you?
    - Would your consistent phenomenal sales performance convict you right off the bat?
    - Or would the ups and downs and inconsistencies of your performance leave plenty of doubt?
- What kind of evidence could be introduced to get you an acquittal?
    - Would there be a completed planner or calendar?
    - Or would the vast empty pages of your calendar prove your innocence?
- What kind of witnesses would be produced?
    - Would you peers introduce evidence of your efficient business conduct?

- Or could a group of customers be produced who could testify that you had the peculiar reputation of managing to get "stuck in traffic" and delayed every time you're supposed to meet with them?

Funny though it might be, this exercise should have generated some thought about the need for improvement. Let's get on with it.

Time Tips

Some ways to get more time are reviewed below.

Dealing with Interruptions

Are you in an office where interruptions are constant? Many hours a week can be wasted by such seemingly harmless questions from passersby that ask you "Got a sec?" Telling them "No" might be what you want to say, but you might also want to be careful, too. Here's a way many find helpful.

Got a sec?

Respond with

"Can we cover it now in under __ minutes, or should we schedule a meeting?"

This is an incredibly simple, polite way to put the onus for the time back on the individual making the request.

Controlling Meetings

Perhaps you are in an office where lots of meetings are called for and held without accomplishing much. An effective way to minimize wasted meetings can be handled using email.

Send out an email to the group that proposes to meet and poll for suggestions as to discussion items; be specific in your questions. Ask the person who called the meeting to circulate an agenda to help you prepare. If they respond and tell you they do not have one, as one is not really required, make a request to handle the meeting by email or by phone.

If you are sent an agenda and are sure you are not required at this meeting, breeze through it, note your thoughts and what you could contribute and send them back. Solicit from the meeting planner any suggestions whereby the meeting could be shortened and held within a defined time limit. Leverage feedback from other members via email as well, if appropriate.

Control Run-on Sales Meetings

Contrary to popular belief, sales meetings with prospects that go on and on are not always in your best interest. Decision makers that are focused and have a plan to execute--which may or may not include buying your solution--are usually not the people who allow meetings to run on. So if you find yourself with people who are letting the meeting run on, you need to take control, but appropriately. The "Town Crier" approach works quite well in these situations.

Wait for an opening in the prospect's 30-minute fishing story and say something like;

"OK, great point, thanks for bringing that up. So, at this point in the meeting, we've covered___."

Or

"I appreciate you taking the first 30 minutes of your time with me to cover that. Can I ask you, how are you for time remaining?"

Oh, I've got another three or four hours for you, Mr. Salesman.

"Well, I've only booked 2 hours for this meeting, Mr. Prospect; but could I make a suggestion?"

Sure.

"For the next 15 minutes, do you mind if we talk about the project timeline and see where we need to go from there? If we need to schedule another meeting to come back, I'd be happy to. Would that work for you?"

OK.

Repeat the process every 15-30 minutes or so until you get your objective for the meeting completed.

Other Time Tips

Make your phone calls first thing in the morning, at lunch and at the last hour of the day. Fewer calls are screened at those hours, most salespeople are not engaged at those times and you can make a lot of calls in three hours per day every day when you normally would be doing something a lot less important.

Wake an hour early. Shut the TV off an hour early. Never use the snooze alarm—set your clock to a later time if necessary, but get UP when it goes off; otherwise you are just practicing procrastination from the very first moment of the day.

Delegate where possible and record everything you do in your ScoreMore™ planner. Looking back on your records is one of the easiest yet most powerful ways to improve your time effectiveness.

Part III: Your Message

Chapter 7: **About Messaging**

What is Messaging?

The message is information you use to convince your prospect of the value of your solution. The core of your sales system is your message. What you say, how you say it, when you say it and why you say it.

Basic Messaging

Ask a room full of salespeople what the strengths of their solution is and you will get a list of answers including things like our "size, age of our company, market share, customer references." Then, ask them to list their weaknesses and you will eventually get a list including things like their "size, age of the company, market share, customer references."

This is not as crazy as it might seem. In many instances the older age, for instance, of the company may be a significant benefit, if they are dealing with a company for whom their older age may say "longevity, conservative, stable." But in other instances of course, the company's older age may say "stodgy, out-moded, and resistant to change."

Knowing your audience is a key factor in messaging successfully. However, salespeople are not marketing people and you do not have the time nor the inclination to sit around all day and study your audience.

So in this Basic Messaging section you are going to learn some elemental truths of messaging for salespeople; as importantly, you are going to learn to apply these in a broad range of instances.

The Fundamentals

In the example you just read about where a room full of salespeople got together in a room and gave the same answers to different questions about their solution's strengths and weaknesses, you were witnessing a phenomenon common in sales messaging. While in that instance, the moderator would be able to spot the obvious problem with their answers and offer some direction, what about in the places where salespeople are messaging for their living and leaving the customer with a question mark over his head or worse, a lack of confidence in their solution?

The fundamental fact of messaging is that any message has different components which need to be combined together in order to make the message compelling.

Errors occur when these elements are mistaken for another; such as in the case of identifying as a strength, the "age" of the company. You saw that the age of the company could imply desirable benefits to one prospect and liabilities to another. The simple fact is that the "age" of the company is neither an asset nor a liability; it is a *fact.*

There are additional basic elements of messaging in addition to facts, which are called *Strategic Value* and *Personal Benefit.* Therefore, the elements of messaging are these;

1. Facts
2. Strategic Values
3. Personal Benefits

Knowing what each of these elements is and how to combine it with the others will revolutionize your sales message.

What are Facts?

Facts are indisputable characteristics of your company and solution. Facts are things like;

- Location
- Size of company
- Balance sheet
- Age of company
- Employee Certification
- # of trained employees
- Type of training
- Information Technology
- Current Infrastructure
- Equipment
- Planned Infrastructure
- Equipment
- Management Experience
- New Management
- Size of facilities

Again, *facts* are not by themselves anything without an interpretation either on the part of the prospect and in his own mind; with the adverse assistance of your competitor; or hopefully, by your sales message first and foremost.

You will see how you can take any *fact* of your competitor's solution or company and turn it into a liability that is more compelling to the prospect than the manner in which your competitor is trying to present it as an asset.

What are Strategic Values?

Strategic values are those items that explain your facts into a compelling reason to do business with you. Strategic Values are things like;

- Increased Revenues
- Decreased Costs
- Fastest
- Highest Quality
- Financial Strength
- Highest Value
- Competitive Advantage
- Low Total Cost Ownership
- Reliability
- Low Risk
- Safety
- Highest Value
- Fastest Service Response
- Opportunity Cost
- Engineering Expertise

Strategic Values cannot be stated by themselves;

- Weak Message: "We have the Fastest Service Response of any provider."

The prospect's response will be one of measured skepticism as they will want to know "how do I know that to be true" since you did not tell them. Contrast this statement with the one below.

- Strong Message: "Due to our location near the interstates of I-285 and I-75 we are able to support our customers with the Fastest Service Response of any provider."

Here, the response must be "Well, that makes sense." Only with an effort can a prospect interpret this statement in any way other than positive.

What are Personal Benefits?

Personal Benefits are the only items that are unique in each situation you may be in.

In other words, you may need to be aware of why your solution is important and how it's going to be used and in what project in order to be able to state with confidence the exact personal benefit which your solution's Facts and Strategic Values are going to bring to prospect "X."

Often, the prospect is considering your solution to fit a particular initiative or project. Every project has parameters and you will need to demonstrate how your solution can fit within those parameters to deliver the project successfully. Or the prospect may have an Executive or Owner who is always interested in meeting certain objectives of the business, be it cost reduction, revenue growth, and profit maximization. By knowing something about the prospect's own situation you can combine statements to hit home runs with your messaging.

Personal Benefits include items like;

- A Cost Cutting Initiative
- A Marketing Program
- A Manufacturing Program
- Legislative Compliance

- A Brainchild of the Owner
- A Pet Project of the Decision Maker

To bring it all the way home for the prospect, you can combine some of the information he has provided to you;

"Due to our location near the interstates of I40 and I75 we are able to support our customers with the Fastest Service Response of any provider; which helps meet your Downtime-Reduction Initiative."

You will use this information when you develop Proof Statements.

Break Down Your Solution

It can be helpful to look at your solution in terms of its individual components. You may or may not ever have a need to describe these individual components to your prospects, but the exercise is often still of great benefit as you go about detailing your winning sales message.

Break down your solution into pieces or sections. What parts of your solution are especially strong? What parts are your customers most impressed with? What part of your solution do you personally like to talk about? Why?

You

You're pretty important to this whole sales messaging thing. So consider your own viewpoint. What are the parts of your solution you feel are really compelling? Why?

If you were in a position to buy your own solution, knowing what you know, would you buy it? Be honest. If the answer is no, you need to realize you either don't have enough information about it and you need to get more; or you do have enough information and you don't believe it's the best solution. In either case, you're not going to be selling very much of it, because you have to believe in what you're selling. Fix your knowledge deficit.

Recent Events

What events have occurred illustrating your solution's success? What new customers have been brought on? Have there been any industry developments that are favorable to you? Any other reports or endorsements?

You really need to stay on top of this type of information as it can be a real windfall. Often, the information your prospect may truly be waiting for is just that someone with his similar problem has had that problem solved by your solution. Keep in regular touch with other salespeople in your company (good, positive salespeople, not any blood-sucking-negative-attitude employees.)

Metrics

Metrics are measurements. They are statistics of your solution's success in your customer environments. Metrics are specific measurable benefits of your solution's bottom line impact. Think in terms of reduced cost, increased profits, increased revenues, increased speed, reduced downtime, etc.

- "ABC Company was able to reduce their costs by 33% after implementing our solution."
- "Customer XYZ was able to increase revenues by 22%..."

The power of metrics is shown by the contrast in the two statements below;

- "XYZ Company has been a satisfied customer for two years now."

vs,

- "XYZ Company has been a satisfied customer for two years now, because they have been able to save 15% on their labor costs on an annual basis which translates into an annual savings of $7.5 million dollars."

Decision Makers are Non-Technical Decision Makers

Lots of sales are held up or lost outright because your recommender or advocate for your solution cannot translate your benefits to the non-technical business decision makers. People in your accounts who are non-technical business decision makers often include people like the CEO and the CFO. If your solution is expensive enough it will always reach their desks. Metrics are a way to quantify your solution's benefits and translate those benefits to non-technical business decision makers.

Applying Your Message

Now that you have reviewed the basics of messaging you can begin to take steps to applying it.

Proof Statements

Proof Statements are powerful elements of your sales message. Proof Statements "prove" your solution's advantages by how you state those advantages. As you have seen, salespeople often handicap their own message by the unfinished manner in which they state their advantages.

Remember that facts are simply facts. They do not lead the prospect to conclude anything other than what he may already believe, which he does not need a salesperson for. Therefore as you have seen, facts like the age of your company can be an asset for one prospect and a liability for another.

Strategic Value is what the prospect is really after. But since he must expect a salesperson to have a bias towards selling, the prospect must balance what he hears from a salesperson with a certain amount of skepticism until he can better validate the truth of the salesperson's statements. As you have seen, therefore, when a salesperson claims his solution will allow the prospect to reduce costs in downtime, for instance, the prospect must balance his own desire to believe the salesperson with a healthy dose of doubt. This keeps him from buying before he has all the facts.

This is a simple example. However, salespeople make the mistake of thinking their statements are being received by the prospect with a high degree of believability when actually the opposite is often true. A prospect is just too professional to allow salespeople to see all of his skepticism. Salespeople need to be as professional in their ability to expect the prospect to be skeptical and craft their sales messaging to compensate.

Proof Statements are one way to accomplish this.

Rather than simply stating that your solution will allow the prospect to reduce his costs in downtime and letting the prospect find a way to believe you, make it easy for him to believe what you've said and difficult to doubt it.

In the Proof Statements exercise in your workbook you are invited to come up with several proof statements. You can do this by drawing from each column heading and arriving at a finished statement. Use the following rules to do so;

Facts prove Strategic Value, which delivers Personal Benefit.

Because of [Fact] we are best able to deliver [Strategic Value.]

Example: Due to our [Balance Sheet] we are uniquely able to deliver [Financial Strength] to your project and the type of [Low Risk & Reliability] your Company Owner demands.

Come up with several of these Proof Statements for your own use.

Customer Scenarios

Customer Scenarios are vital elements for strong sales messaging. As you have seen, customer success is one of the most important sales tools you have to sell your solution to new prospects.

Use your workbook to develop customer scenarios that can be used in applying your sales message.

Competitive Messaging

Messaging against your competition can be done effectively if you take care how you use it. Be accurate in your descriptions, because competitive statements can come back like a boomerang. Begin with a careful analysis of their strengths and weaknesses. Where are they strong and why? What are their weaknesses and why?

You

Again, consider your own viewpoint. Based on what you understand about your competition put yourself in the position of buying the solution. What fears would you have about doing so? How would you feel about purchasing their solution? Why would you feel that way? How would you go about arming yourself with information to defeat their solution?

Recent Events

What events have occurred where the competition failed or came up short? What customers or references allowed you to gain this information? Would they be willing to give you more information about these failures? Would they be willing to give your prospects this information?

Competitive Proof Statements

Assemble some competitive proof statements. Use the same process as you used to assemble your own proof statements. Select Facts, combine them with Strategic Flaws and attach them to Personal Benefits.

Because of [Fact] they are unable to deliver [Strategic Value.] Example: "ABC Company suspects it was because of my competition's [recent loss of key personnel] that caused the [increase in downtime] which forced ABC to [lose a $12 million sale to the DOD.]"

Using this approach will help you to phrase powerful statements exposing your competition's weaknesses—information which it is your duty to share with the prospect.

Chapter 8: **Elevator Message**

What is the Elevator Message?

The Elevator Message is a brief 30-second commercial for your solution delivered in-person that causes the prospect to ask "Can you do that for me?"

Once crafted, salespeople can use this message in dozens of other situations from presentations and letters to prospecting phone calls.

Your Elevator Message

This term comes from the main situation where it's used; finding out you're in an elevator with the CEO or key contact from a prospects company. He is going to be getting off at some floor within a few moments; if you want him to remember you, you've got to have something to say which creates an impact.

That situation typifies many that salespeople are often faced with. An opportunity--large or small--presents itself and you need to capitalize on it inside of just a few moments. This happens often enough though surprisingly very few salespeople are prepared to deal with it.

The Result You Want

"Can you do that for me?"

This is the key question you want your prospect to be coming back at you with. What you've said has made him think that if he doesn't talk with you he's nuts. Does your elevator message do that now?

The Good, Bad and Ugly of Messages

It can help you to consider some examples of elevator messages that do and do not work well.

The Gabber Message

This message type is a favorite of salespeople and is termed the "Gabber" for obvious reasons.

- "Hi Mr. Prospect, I hope you're doing great today. How're the kids? The wife? Been doing much golfing? Fishing? That reminds me of the time when I was up on Lake Wannahockaloogie and I caught a sturgeon that almost capsized my canoe…did I mention that I canoe? Been doing it for years, even been in some whitewater before—but don't get me talking about politics HAR! HAR! Anyway what I'm doing now is I got started in this job on account of what I thought would be a good business to get into—I figured I could really help people, see? So I figure, by helping you, you might help me, see how that works? And I thought, well...."

Don't be a Gabber.

The Take it or Leave it Message

The "Take It or Leave It" message is a favorite among the self-proclaimed elite of the sales profession.

- "I'm in pharmaceuticals."
- "I'm in financial services."
- "I'm a recruiter."

Invest more in your message than this guy does.

The Buffet Table Message

The "Buffet Table" message is similar to the "Gabber" in length, but has some redeeming qualities in that it is confined to business benefits; the problem with it is that the prospect is left to link the benefits together himself and often just doesn't.

"Can I tell you what I do? I work with those companies—like yours—that might want to obtain an improvement in operational efficiency, particularly as regards their payroll and HR functions. We focus on the unique demands of your company culture by applying Neuro Linguistic Programming, Dynamic Job Matching and extra-sensory simulation to identify trends in your environment which might lead to over-stress, high employee attrition or even marked increase in employee litigation. This is a program which we have successfully implemented and in over 90% of those cases saw a marked drop in the volume of costly settlements."

The Elevator Message

The "Elevator Message" in its true form makes a high impact statement in a minimum amount of time.

"I work with companies that are concerned with reducing excessive problems and costs associated with employee attrition and even litigation. Our HR audit will point to immediate issues which you can implement—on your own—to reduce these costly issues. We've just done one at ABC Company and saved them $120,000. As a matter of fact, if our audit doesn't save you 5 times what it costs, it's FREE."

Message Components

Breaking down the Elevator Message into its components will help you in crafting your own.

Message Framework

The framework around which you describe your message is important. It should be logical, captivating and leave the customer with the inclination to wonder; "Can you do that for me?"

- ✓ Hook. I work with companies who want to ______;
- ✓ Reference. Customers such as ____;
- ✓ Body. What we do for them is to allow them to ___;
- ✓ Metric. For instance [XYZ] was able to save $000/ and avoid a painful situation with [insert nightmare.]

The Hook

The first part of the elevator message is the Hook. Its purpose is to engage the prospect into the message. Here you draw a picture for him of the conditions that bring your customers to you, such as unique problems, costs and challenges within certain aspects of their business. Those statements are best preceded by the statement as follows;

"I work with companies who... [have the following conditions.]"

In order to complete the rest of the Hook, ask yourself questions like;

- ✓ What do you sell?
- ✓ How does your company make money?
- ✓ Why does your customer pay out money for your solution?

The Reference

The second piece is called the Reference.

The purpose of the reference is to establish credibility that customers have used your solution successfully before.

"Companies like... [insert customer names.]"

Ask yourself;

- ✓ Who are some of your top customers?
- ✓ How long have they been a customer?

Be sure you are well versed in the customer you are referencing in the event the prospect asks you further questions about them.

The Body

The third piece of the message is the Body.

Its purpose is to state key benefits that should appeal to the prospect's need. You should insert the benefit statements regarding your solution, its impact, the changes it brings, and the set of great things that happens to whomever is smart enough to acquire that solution.

"What we do for them is to allow them to... [insert a positive set of experiences.]"

Ask yourself;

- ✓ What does your solution do for your prospect?
- ✓ How does it help them save money?
- ✓ Does it make money for your prospect?
- ✓ Is there a nightmare situation your solution removes?

The Metric

The final piece is called the Metric piece, because while it is not mandatory, if delivered appropriately it can be very effective.

The purpose of the Metric piece is to establish additional credibility by spelling out a specific customer experience and reference. It's important to be mindful of the time when doing this so as to avoid running too long.

"For instance... [XYZ Company experienced the following.]"

A Finished Example

"I work with sales management to grow the effectiveness of their sales teams by keeping score, cutting cost and selling more. We do this by penetrating the cloud that obscures visibility into the value of the sales team's activities. We help set up metrics to keep score, reduce cost by ditching bad behaviors and help them sell more through strong optimized sales process and strategy. For instance at XYZ, we were able to grow new business acquisition over 360% while they simultaneously reduced sales payroll by over 55%."

Part IV: Prospecting

Chapter 9: About Prospecting

Prospecting is selling. Prospecting successfully is selling successfully. Many a timid, stammering, poor presenter and lousy closer were awarded the "Sales Performer of the Year" at their company entirely due to their prospecting skills.

What is Prospecting

Prospecting is the act of reaching out to a contact or company to begin the process of selling.

What Prospecting is Not

Driving around looking to make a cold call, sorting through databases or phone number lists, or anything else where you are getting ready to prospect.

Why You Should Learn to be Great at Prospecting

Prospecting is the lifeblood of the sales business. Your ability to find high quality prospects for your solution is the single most important capability you have as a professional salesperson.

Being great in prospecting is going to make you more effective at getting the appointments you need to make the sales you need.

Being great in prospecting is going to make your selling so much easier, with fewer problems as you will be able to pick and choose the accounts you want to sell to out of the larger pool of prospects that effective prospecting delivers to you.

What is Fun about Prospecting

You Can Prospect Anywhere

With cell phones and wireless you can prospect anywhere, in your car, at your house, outdoors, in a cafe.

You Can Prospect Anytime

You can leave voicemails in the middle of the night if you need to. You can utilize cell phones to prospect from your car on the way to an appointment, on the way back from an appointment, on the way to work, on the way home. You can prospect in the middle of the night into voicemail, reach busy decision makers in early morning hours or even on Saturday mornings.

You Can Prospect Yourself, Delegate Some of it or All of it

Most salespeople prospect themselves (why pay someone else to do it when you can have all the fun doing it yourself?) With practice you will find yourself outpacing even the most experienced inside sales teams your company offers. And there is nothing like the exhilaration added to your sales day to be adding a few key appointments in those Target Accounts!

But there are times when you will not be able to handle all of the prospecting that you would like to have done, in which case outsourcing the task is an option. Use either a firm specializing in prospecting or you can hire an employee to do it for you if the right one comes along.

You Can Prospect by Phone, by Letter, by Email

There is no reason to become over attached or even bored with any single method of prospecting when there is more than one way to prospect. Utilizing more than one medium—phone, letter, email—is a great way to grab and hold the prospects attention long enough to get the introductory meeting.

You Can Prospect Manually or Automate it Using Technology

You can handle the task of prospecting—in whatever form you choose—or you can automate the task using emails and some advanced technology and services to assist you.

Prospecting is an Immediate Measurement of Your Sales Effectiveness

It is the most easily measured part of the sales process and always yields to one thing more than any other; hard work. The more you prospect, the more effective your prospecting will be. The more people you contact, the higher the number (if not the percentage) that will agree to meet with you. Of course the more that meet with you, the more you have a chance to sell to, and the higher the number (if not the percentage) of your sales transactions.

For example if you make 50 calls today and get 5 appointments you know you have a 10% prospecting success rate. Also, you can plug in your average revenue value per phone call or average commission per appointment and see that every call you make earns you money.

Numbers vs. Percentages

Prospecting numbers are about how many phone calls, how many contacts, how many appointments set. Prospecting percentages are about how many phone calls you need to make to get one appointment. If you need to make 100 calls to get one appointment, your percentage of success in phone calls is 1.0%.

In prospecting, both numbers and percentages are of course important. But of the two, the one to be most careful about is the numbers. Make sure you are doing ENOUGH calls every day, every week to get enough of the appointments you need to make the number of sales you need to make and you will be fine.

Percentage of success comes in as you want to track effectiveness and improve that effectiveness. Like all great sports statistics, watching your percentage of success improve in prospecting is both motivational and also indicative of how effective whatever new approach you are using actually is.

Chapter 10: **Compression Prospecting**

Winners Make More Calls

Winners make more calls is a plain, simple and age old truth of the successful salesperson. Salespeople who are able to manage themselves to make more calls on purpose and to make better use of their downtime by either filling it with making more calls or preparing themselves to make more calls are salespeople that are on their way to top production (if they are not already there.)

What is Compression Prospecting?

Compression Prospecting is about maximizing your ability to touch more prospects, more often, more effectively and faster. You make more calls, to more prospects and use tools to help you where necessary. Above all Compression Prospecting is about attitude—you do it because you want more success.

Why It Works

Compression Prospecting never fails. Selling is still a numbers game at its most elemental and you can be reasonably sure it always will be.

Prospects almost never respond on the first contact. They are often too busy to take your call or are out of the office or in a meeting. You need to be able to identify those prospects that are not responding because they are too busy from those prospects that are not responding because they are not actually prospects at all. And since they are not going to call you, you need to be ready to contact them. And to call them back as many times as you deem necessary.

Face it—you never make calls because you feel like making calls. You make calls because you need appointments and meetings with prospects who can make a decision for your solution. That's it; so don't wait around till you feel like it, because you never will.

It Takes More Calls Than Ever to be Successful in Prospecting

Compression Prospecting is a practice of calling enough to overcome the obstacles to traditional prospects; things like gatekeepers, voicemail, prospects who are unavailable. That was why Compression Prospecting was important in the past.

But people are busier than ever in today's world. While the preferred method of communication for prospects in the past was the phone today it's email. In the past you could get a phone number from anyone—try getting his or her email today. So while email is the preferred method of communication, you still need to prospect primarily by phone. This means that salespeople have to be ready to make even more calls than in the past to overcome all the normal obstacles plus all the new obstacles.

More Benefits of Compression Prospecting

Being able to prospect more effectively to more prospects means you will have more opportunities to sell and acquire more customers and more of the best quality customers.

Compression prospectors miss out on much of the grief associated with selling. They do not have as much trouble getting appointments to sell. They do not have to deal with the troubles of selling to contacts that do not have the ability to make a decision. They have faster and shorter sales cycles, because they get a jump on the sales process by selecting whom they want to sell to and when. They enjoy high-level sponsorship in the organizations they sell to because they seek it and get it more often than not. Compression prospectors do not struggle to hit their sales targets because they are always generating high quality leads for themselves rather than stressing out over how to sell to the poor quality leads that any salesperson gets.

Compression prospectors make it happen for themselves. If they want a higher number of customers, they contact a higher number of prospects. If they want a higher profit margin in their transactions, they call more prospects and qualify the ones capable of delivering that margin.

Exposing Call Reluctance

A Discipline of Compression Prospecting will Prevent this Problem

The biggest problem with sales in general and prospecting in particular is that salespeople simply do not do enough of it. Having a proactive discipline of Compression Prospecting will help you avoid falling victim to this biggest problem of all—that salespeople simply do not prospect enough.

Free Telemarketing Service

To illustrate this fact, imagine that one of the benefits you now have is a free telemarketing service being done by a highly qualified retired telemarketer who only wants the satisfaction of working hard for you.

He is willing to call for you for two hours every day. How many calls would you expect him to make per hour—remember he is a top producing telemarketing agent. 10? Way too low. 15? Better. 20 is more like it.

Now, how many appointments would you expect him to set for you? Out of twenty calls per hour—1? 2? More?

And how many appointments do you need on average to get one sale? If one of five prospects becomes a customer for you, then this telemarketer will be supplying you with one net new sale per week, so long as he produces one qualified appointment from each day's calling activities.

Suppose now that this telemarketer comes to you at the end of the quarter and asks for a fair wage to continue working with you. If he had been finding you one new sale per week, or even just one new sale every two weeks or even one per month--what would you be willing to pay him for his services?

There is one thing that emerges from this fictional exercise; the fact that there is *real* value to Compression Prospecting. Compression Prospecting is not the "if" most call-reluctant salespeople have made it to be—it's the "when." Compression Prospecting will do more for you and your sales career than any other single discipline ever will.

And that's a fact.

Compression Prospecting in Your World

The more calls you make, the better off you are. So how many prospecting phone calls is it possible to make? For example, taking 100 prospects and calling them each 3 times is 300 calls. How long should it take for someone to do this? Get ready.

In one hour you should be able to dial the phone 15-17 times, leaving enough time to have one or two business conversations with the one or two prospects that answer. By business conversation is meant the discussion between a salesperson looking to qualify a prospect and a prospect answering those qualifying questions.

Five Minute Discussions

You will have all kinds and type of prospects, some nice, some not—but on the average a business discussion should not take more than 5 to 10 minutes to qualify an appointment (not to attempt to sell someone on doing business with your company!) Most salespeople have no appreciation for time and therefore no real reason to be brief, focused and business like in their discussions with their prospects. After all, they reason, I called him, if he wants to chatter on about something it's my polite responsibility to listen. Wrong. It's your responsibility to set the appointment and get back to prospecting.

Back to our example. If it takes you an hour to make 15-17 calls, you can make 45-51 calls every three hours and a full 150 calls within 9 hours of work. Condensed, that's one work day.

If you took the time to make calls during times of the day during which most salespeople are sleeping, eating or loafing you could do all these calls and still have some left over. For instance, look at the hours of 7:00 am (sleeping); noon (eating) and 5:00 pm (loafing.) There are 15 of those hours in every week. If you are like most salespeople they are currently unused hours. (Remember what you could earn if you could put three hours per day to work for you? See the chart in the chapter on Time Management.) Putting those hours to work for you by making calls means you could touch at least 15 prospects per hour; which are 225 calls on prospects per week that you currently are not making.

3 hours x 5 days = 15 hours x 15 calls = 225 calls.

All these calls will work against the natural challenges facing salespeople today. The more attempts you make on your market, the more opportunity, which equals more results over the long run yes, but you will be pretty well pleased with what you see happen over the short run with as well.

For what it's worth I have never seen Compression Prospecting fail to generate considerable value to the salesperson that applies it. So, separate yourself from the naysayers, the negative talks, and the water cooler Monday morning quarterbacks and from sales failure—hit Compression Prospecting and hit it with all you've got.

More Tips for Compression Prospecting

When to Call

Whenever you can, but its best to call when decision makers are at their desks and able to receive your call. The early morning hours of 7 am, the noon hours when everyone is at lunch and the hours immediately after the workday at 5 pm are good times to target.

VIP Calls

When you are making calls to VIPs—those people who are either high up in the organization or who are exceptionally significant—make sure to make a few calls to other lower priority prospects first. Speaking takes muscles and you want those muscles warmed up; no sense choking over "morning-tongue" if you can help it. Also, using landlines rather than cell phones to make those calls means less chance of interference or disconnecting.

Cell phones

The one rule with cell phones is "use 'em." Call in the car on the way to the appointment and on the way back from the appointment; call going to work and going home; call and call and call. Get a good smart phone so all your contacts are on it and organized into groups by industry or by customer or both.

Voicemail

Voicemail is something we will get into in more detail later on. But for now some points of value are helpful.

Always leave a complete message, even if you say something wrong or need to edit it—always complete the message first, then go back and edit the message using the available prompts. As many salespeople have found out the hard way, sometimes the voicemail system is not as forgiving as they had hoped. For instance, a salesperson makes a mistake leaving his message, abruptly stops talking and tries to use the prompts to edit the message; only the prompts are different on this particular system and the voicemail is left as is, half complete, with stutters, errors and all—right on the prospects voicemail. Nice impression of professionalism, eh? Avoid this problem by completing your message—any mistake you make simply treat as if you were talking live to the prospect, correcting it with a simple "excuse me, what I meant to say was--" and complete the message. Edit afterwards.

Finally, regarding voicemail, leave your number twice; the first time at normal conversational pace, though of course very clearly, the second time far slower and more deliberately to allow the prospect time to write it down.

Closing for the Meeting

Ok, so you make the call to the prospect; he answers and says he is in a meeting, or busy or simply cannot talk right now, but tells you to "call back."

One of the biggest problems with setting the meetings with your prospects comes in the last few inches; when you have the prospect on the phone and sometimes even ready to schedule the meeting, but something delays that from happening. And the salesperson gets off the phone, intending to follow up and either doesn't, or when he does follow up he finds the prospect unavailable, or has forgotten and is no longer interested, etc.

Another error salespeople resort to in order to avoid the above situation is to try to force the prospect to hear you out;

- "Mr. Prospect this will only take a second…"

All you have to do is try that a few times to see how poor a solution that is.

The problem is, when the prospect says to "call back," what most salespeople do is they rush to accommodate the prospect. In a hurry. As a matter of fact, the salesperson becomes so much in a hurry that whatever hurry the prospect was in initially is way slow by comparison with the blur at which salespeople speedily accommodate the prospect, believing by so doing, they are either avoiding getting yelled at or are possibly earning points with the prospect as they show how accommodating they can be. After all, the prospect said to call back and you don't want him to change his mind do you?

Nonsense.

Slow Down

You are an important person with an important message, right? The prospect has a real benefit to gain by hearing you out, right? Now might not be the best time to talk with the prospect as he has just said he cannot talk to you at the moment, but he has said to call back and you are under obligation to believe he actually means it.

But, when should you call back? You need to get that information to avoid pointlessly chasing the prospect. Do not try this;

- "Mr. Prospect, would you be able to let me know what might be a good time in which to return the call? I'd hate to have to call back more than once and leave a number of messages and…"

It's too wordy for the situation.

Some slick sales training actually suggests;

- "Mr. Prospect, in order to avoid playing phone tag, why don't we set an appointment?

What kind of a veiled threat is that, anyway? You're telling the prospect you are going to call him back and miss him and he is going to call you back and miss you. What reason does he have to call you back in the first place? And he just said now is not the time—why are you pushing?

Handling Delays

No, the key to getting the callback time is to make the request invisible and you do that by speaking exactly as he is—in clipped, busy-businessman tones.

So when the prospect says

Can't talk—in a meeting right now; call me back.

You say,

"When?"

That's it.

He tosses out a non specific;

Tomorrow.

Now what? Well, keep going. You respond with;

"What time?"

He says;

Anytime.

You say;

"Any time's that won't work?"

He says;

Yes, not before 9 am.

You say;

"Talk to you then, thanks, bye."

You may say that's going too far—not at all. You're doing what he asked and you're helping him. You're clearing the clutter calls he could be getting from you, the voicemails and meeting interruptions. You are behaving as he would expect a valued professional to behave with his own time. All in about 10 seconds. Look again;

"*Call back*—when?—*Tomorrow*—what time?—*Anytime*—any times that won't work?—*Yes, not before 9 am.*"

Keeping it short, real short and just like it is, keeps his mind off the fact that you have some stupid sales pitch to bore him with and lets him know you are a busy professional who can at the very least recognize when someone like him is in a hurry and respond to it appropriately.

Try it.

The Pencil-In Appointment Close

Another common problem or barrier to getting the meeting scheduled is a delay, as when a prospect has to double-check with other people's schedules or when he needs to confirm his own availability after checking on another commitment.

Prospect says; "*I'd like to meet, but I need to check on my monthly project meeting with the team.*"

Typically, salespeople say "OK, I'll call back" and the meeting flies into oblivion.

Instead, try the Pencil-In meeting close.

When the prospect says; "*I'd like to meet, but I need to check on my monthly project meeting with the team.*"

- ✓ "I understand—let me make a suggestion. Why don't we pencil-in a convenient time and I will follow up a few days before to confirm it still works."

Prospect says;

OK, sure.

Dealing with More Delays

There are additional forms of delays you will see prospects using.

I am out this week and next.

Now this is either an attempt to stall you or is a simple matter of fact. Either way, you can answer it simply;

"So, we're looking at the week after next. How does Tuesday look?"

The power in these responses and their effectiveness with the prospect is in that they are immediate responses and are simple and so they tend to not activate the prospects' sales defenses.

Another delay may seem particularly daunting inasmuch as it seems almost unreasonable to respond to when in fact it is one of the easiest from which to schedule an appointment.

Prospect says;

I am booked through next month.

WOW. How do you come back to that one? Simple!

✓ "OK, I'm booking out to June right now. Why don't we pencil in a time six weeks out and follow up beforehand to confirm?

Half the time the prospect will agree to do this, because it's reasonable and his schedule is open when looked at that far out. It's important that you remain relaxed and credible when you deliver this. Recall that you are not claiming to have a full schedule out that far, but that you are booking appointments out that far, which is true, because you *are* booking appointments that far out.

Geography and Name Dropping

These next appointment closes work by taking advantage of a psychological fact that familiarity is persuasive. Leverage familiarity by referencing in both geographical and in social terms and you can have more success in persuading a prospect to accept an appointment with you.

Geography

The Same Town geographic close works when you are planning to be in the same town as the prospect. For a prospect that is in New York;

"I am going to be in New York the week after next. Why don't we get together then?"

It even works with different towns! For the same prospect;

"I am going to be in Tampa next week; why don't we get together the week after?"

I am not exactly sure why that is, it may be that you sound like a mover and shaker; anyone that travels that much is probably in demand and there is an incentive on the part of the prospect to accept the appointment as a scarce commodity. As a technique it's only here because it works.

Name Dropping

Another way to establish familiarity is by using references of current customers or prospects. The interesting thing to note is you can establish familiarity without having to reference actual customers but just companies who are considering doing business with you and are, at this point, simply a prospect for your solution, just like the person you are calling. This is especially helpful to those salespeople who work for start-ups without many customers yet.

"I'll be meeting with one of our current customers--ABC Company--next Wednesday; why don't we get together after that?"

If ABC Company is still only a prospect;

"I'll be meeting with ABC Company for the first time as well next Wednesday; why don't we get together after that?"

While this is not as powerful as if ABC Company were a customer, it still adds familiarity to the request. Since your solution is new, not many companies would have had a chance to buy it yet, but it is still good to know that other companies the prospect is familiar with are considering it and that he is in good company to meet with you as well.

Pre-Email

Another way to increase the effectiveness when closing for appointments is to use email. In this case you have spoken to this individual before and are following up (he gave you his email right?)

A very simple form of email called Pre-Email is used here to let the prospect know you will be calling so that when you actually do call, there is an aspect of familiarity to the call. He does not have to grope in his mind for why you are calling.

The Pre-Email is written similar to this;

- "Hi Joe;
- I hope you've been well. I just wanted to let you know I will be calling you in the next day or so to see about our discussion. Feel free to let me know if that's ok; I look forward to speaking."

When the prospect knows to expect your call, you get higher visibility or recognition in their all-important mindshare category. If he knows you're calling, he might be less likely to screen that caller id number he doesn't recognize.

When the phone rings he may only have a vague recollection that someone notified him they're going to be calling. But that's all you need. And since very few people of un-importance let other people know when they're going to call and since you value your time enough to take steps to give him advance notice of your call, you automatically, irrevocably force his mind to accept that you are in fact important.

All this works in your favor and increases the chance he'll pick up when you call. Alternatively, he may just let you know that you need to call him at a more convenient time, which you'll be more than happy to do.

Tri-Touch

Tri-Touch is a technique that enhances the visibility of your communication to the prospect.

Essentially, it works by using a significant communication (letter, proposal, etc.) to send multiple communications to the prospect. Handled correctly, Tri-Touch is a powerful way to get your message the attention it deserves.

Here's how it works. Suppose you want to send information about a new product release to your prospect. In the old days, simply sending it would be sufficient. Today, with all the information flooding your prospect's desk and pc, it takes more to avoid having your information lost in the shuffle.

You could place a call to the prospect, most likely getting voicemail, and leave a message about the information you will be sending out, what it is about and why it might have an interest to the prospect.

You then send the information out to the prospect, by email or postal mail.

Finally, you follow up with the prospect via email or phone, thanking him for receiving the information, reaffirming why it might be of interest to him and committing to follow up with him to ask his opinion of it at a later time.

The benefits of using these three points of contact instead of just one is—if handled correctly—it allows you to increase high value contacts with the prospect, instead of settling for one hit-or-miss contact with the prospect. As you will continue to see, the more points of valued contact made with the prospect, the more certain you can be that you stand a good chance of being received when it is time to sell to that prospect.

Handling Cancellations

You have taken the right steps in getting the appointment set and now you get an email cancellation.

I can't meet with you as planned, we will need to re-schedule, thanks.

How do you keep your meeting on track, even if the prospect cannot keep the original date?

Many salespeople call the prospect right back, leave a voicemail, send an email, call and call until they get the prospect on the phone who tells them—you guessed it—"I can't meet with you, we will need to schedule, thanks." Only they may be a little irritable with you now, wondering why you need to hammer them even after they sent you an email message.

Or the salesperson might sit back and wait for the prospect to get in touch with them. It's amazing how many salespeople justify this lame approach as being the higher-road to take. Higher or lower, it ends in no-sale.

So what do you do? You begin where they left off and you send the following campaign of messages, each carefully crafted to allow for persistence without being abrasive.

- ✓ Email
- ✓ Call / Voicemail
- ✓ Call
- ✓ Repeat

The first is the email message.

Email response to cancellation

- ✓ "Thanks for your message; I appreciate you taking the time to let me know. I look forward to meeting at some point in the near future. In that light and for your convenience I will be in touch at x-time to reschedule. If that won't work, feel free to let me know, thanks."

Be deliberate about the date you will be following up with them. If it works for you to immediately follow up by phone, take the next step immediately, however it's often advisable to wait a day or so if you're unsure.

Voicemail response to cancellation

- ✓ "Hi, this is [name]. Just calling to reschedule. I understand that you're unavailable. I will be in touch before the day's out. If you need to call me I am at (phone number.) Otherwise, I look forward to speaking."

Connecting by Phone

Once they do pick up the phone, you can simply greet them and let them know you are following up to reschedule the appointment they needed to cancel. You do not need to reference the communications you sent, why they cancelled, or anything else. Simply state why you are calling, secure the appointment and get off the phone. Remember to use the appointment closes we just covered to help since your prospect may drop into natural resistance again.

More Tips

Stopper Technique

If your business is stereotyped and highly competitive with a high level of prospect prejudice, use the Stopper

Technique. The Stopper Technique is a brief introduction followed by;

"Should I stop there?"

Example:

- ✓ "I'm a Sales Trainer—should I stop there?"
- ✓ "I am in Employee Benefits; should I stop there?"

This relaxes prospect by giving them 'control' over the call and allows you the time you need to get the appointment.

Increase Pickups

The Double Call

Call and if no answer hang up and call back immediately. This works if you do not overuse it.

Re "What's this in reference to?"

Use this when the secretary screens your call.

"I am calling about a recent conversation I had with Ford Motor Corp (or some local large company.)"

Vary it with one of their local Big Customers (confirm who their customers are by speaking with their sales group first) or major competitor.

Paging

Press "0" from his voicemail and ask for your contact to be paged. Ask if he is still in the office? Plan your next call accordingly.

Transfer Request

Call back to the Executive Office or CEO's office and ask for them to transfer you again. This will show on the prospect's caller ID and he is more likely to pick up.

Extension Variation

Try calling versions of the prospect's extension. For example if their actual extension is 2400, try 2401, 2402, etc. When the other person picks up, say "I'm sorry, I'm trying to reach Joe Prospect—could you transfer me? Thanks."

Peer Confirmation

Call back to the Referring Person (MR. Big) if you not getting anywhere and confirm you are doing what he recommended you to do. He may offer you some advice, give you someone else to contact, or go kick his guy in the can to return your call.

Cold call other Executives

Review their website for other names of executives. Call the main switchboard and use the dial by name to get to him on the phone. Request his help or a transfer.

Try Calling at Different Times

Try AM, PM, Noon.

The Most Powerful Appointment Setting Technique Ever

This is an appointment setting technique that requires you to already have the First Meeting set with the prospect. It belongs in this discussion because it can really be effective in keeping your schedule full of good meetings with the prospect.

Set the Follow Up Meeting

How much time does it take you to set a follow up meeting with your prospect? In other words, you have a meeting with the prospect, it goes well, you both agree to perform some intermediate work on your own, and then get back together at some point in the near future to compare notes, hold a demonstration, review a proposal, etc.

How long does it take you to set that appointment? Most times you will need to re-enter the chase again, making phone calls, leaving voicemails, sending emails. Then you make contact, the prospect tries to remember what it was you were going to talk about and you are faced with re-selling him.

There is a much easier, more effective way.

How to Set the Appointment Before You Leave

Begin the meeting by including your intention to ask for the next meeting—make it part of your introductory remarks.

"Thanks for taking the time to meet with me today. What I was hoping to do was talk about what my company does; learn what's important to you and see where we go from there. If it makes sense, perhaps we can schedule our next meeting before I leave? That's up to you."

Close the Meeting with the Request

"Thanks for taking the time with me today."

"Are you open to setting a time for me to come back with _____?" for instance if you have some deliverable out of your discussion, such as some additional information, a proposal etc.

You can also make it a simple lunch request;

"Are you open for lunch the week after next?"

Objections or Stalls

If the prospect objects, or feels he needs to check with someone else, or wait to see the information, etc., treat it just like you would if you were on the phone. Consider the appointment closes you read earlier.

For example, after you ask to set the meeting, the prospect says;

"I'll need to check with John and get back to you."

You can say;

"Of course, that makes sense—why don't we pencil in a time and I will give you a call later to confirm it works?"

Chapter 11: **Calling High**

What is Calling High?

Calling High is about contacting the highest relevant person in the organization; Mr. Big.

Why Call Mr. Big

Mr. Big can help you get further ahead with your sale than anyone else in the organization. Mr. Big is the agenda setter for the organization. If he wants someone in his company to meet with you, they will do it.

When you call Mr. Big you can get information that his subordinates don't have as it pertains to your solution. Additionally, you cannot be ignored by whomever he sends you to; no subordinate or VP will ignore you if Mr. Big refers you to them. And you can gain a peer basis with the VPs and other offices of the company for the simple reason that they are the only ones who have regular conversations with Mr. Big.

Another reason you want to call on Mr. Big is that so few salespeople ever try to call him, so you are way ahead of your competition when you get him on the phone.

Objections to Calling Mr. Big

Many salespeople are just plain afraid to call on Mr. Big and try unsuccessfully to mask their fear by making up silly reasons why they should not be calling him in the first place. Some even claim that Mr. Big is simply "too big" for what they sell—whatever that means. Others suggest that subordinates will resent you and resist you if you get referred down by Mr. Big, which can be somewhat true, but since those subordinates resent anyone that isn't their incumbent, you're still better off starting with Mr. Big.

Types of High Level Calls

There are three types of calls with respect to calling high, depending on who answers the phone; you will want to know how to address each one of them.

- ✓ Mary Powers: what to say to the secretary.
- ✓ Mr. Big: what to say to Mr. Big
- ✓ The EIO: what to say to the Executive Initiative Owner.

Preparing for the Call

When calling Mr. Big you need to have something good to say. The Executive Reference Statement will help you do that.

Executive Reference Statement

The Executive Reference Statement, or ERS, is the mini-commercial for your solution. The ERS will address Mr. Big's hot points as they relate to your solution's benefits.

What are Mr. Big's hot points?

- ✓ Business Improvement—growth, profit
- ✓ Competitiveness, survival
- ✓ Cost Reduction

As you can see Mr. Big's hot points have everything to do with big picture business issues. They have very little to do with the features of your solution. Do not make the mistake of attempting to impress Mr. Big with your grasp of the technical features and capabilities of your solution. You will lose his interest fast. Instead boil down your solution to the business gains that your solution provides to your customers.

Your ERS could run as follows;

- ✓ "We provide solutions which…"
  - Lower costs OR increase profitability OR increase revenue
  - By how much %
- ✓ "We do this by…"
  - Automating OR eliminating OR improving OR enabling *something*
- ✓ "We've done this for companies like…"
  - ABC and XYZ.
- ✓ "I am calling to…"
  - Set an appointment with you to discuss…

When you call Mr. Big, your ERS is what you are going to use to earn his attention, his respect and his interest.

- Attention
- Respect
- Interest

You earn his attention by being focused, professional and brief. You earn his respect by sounding like an expert in what you do and proficient in what you can do for him. You earn his interest by the good sense behind your suggested next step.

You can take your ERS and apply it for use in each of the three types of calls mentioned earlier.

Sample ERS

"My company provides solutions which can cut sales costs in half and still grow new business revenue from 200-400%. We do this by a combination of sales training and automated sales management reporting. We did this for XYZ Corp who cut sales payroll costs by 55% and still grew new business acquisition by over 367% in less than six months."

Call Type 1: the Not-the-Gatekeeper Call

The first call is also the most common. Most often when you call high you will end up speaking to Mr. Big's secretary. This happens so often it is truly amazing to see how many salespeople use approaches that are demeaning or dismissive to this vital person in Mr. Big's organization.

This is also called the "Not-the-Gatekeeper" call because that tired, old way of referring to Mr. Big's secretary as the Gatekeeper helps salespeople to take the wrong attitude in speaking with her. Instead you can think of her as human and a pretty important one, too; Mary Powers.

Facts about Mary Powers

Mary has power. The bigger the organization she works for, the more power she has.

She is a vital person to Mr. Big and he depends upon her. She is responsible for representing him to anyone from the outside world that is contacting Mr. Big by phone.

She is the Voice of the Company

Mr. Big deals with a lot of other Mr. Bigs and sooner or later they all deal in some way with Mary Powers. The people who call Mr. Big are people like his professional peers, the board of directors and outside investors to name just a very few.

She is paid very well for what she does, because people who can do what she can do and do it well are very rare and in high demand. Keeping that in mind will help you to adopt the proper attitude in speaking with her.

She is responsible for protecting Mr. Big's time. She does not accomplish this by being a witch to the people who call; quite the opposite. She does this by carefully and politely qualifying them. She knows who needs to speak to Mr. Big and how to route anyone who does not need to speak to him in the right direction.

If you are able to help Mr. Big, she not only knows *how* to help you--she *will* help you, if you know how to ask.

May I Have the Office of Mr. Big

Call the company's main phone number and when the answering system picks up press zero for the operator.

XYZ Corporation.

"May I have the office of Mr. Big please?"

Asking for the office of Mr. Big is way different than asking for Mr. Big himself. The first will get you transferred, the second may get you screened right there at the front desk.

At the Office of Mr. Big

Mr. Big's office, Mary Powers speaking.

"Hi Mary, this is Kevin Leveille, calling from Score Selling. How are you today?"

(Your introduction is simple; identify yourself and be polite.)

I'm fine. How are you?

Getting Pointed in the Right Direction

"I'm fine, thank you. Mary, I'm just trying to get pointed in the right direction at XYZ Corporation; would you be able to help me?"

I'll try.

Mary will try because part of Mary's job is to get people pointed in the right direction at XYZ Corporation. Also, you didn't try anything fishy by asking to speak to Mr. Big, but instead are speaking directly to her. This approach shows her the proper respect for her position and regard for what she can do for you.

Do I Need to Meet with Mr. Big?

"Great. What my company does is this; (insert your Executive Reference Statement here.) Now, I don't know if I need to be meeting with Mr. Big about this, do you?"

No, I don't think so. A better person would be Joe Sampson, our Chief Sales Officer.

When you ask Mary her opinion there are two outcomes; one is she will most likely refer you to someone who works for Mr. Big and the rest of our discussion here assumes that outcome. But, she may also surprise you by saying;

Yes, you do need to speak with him about this. Would you like to schedule a meeting?

An Alternative Request

An alternative to asking Mary her opinion about meeting with Mr. Big is if you know the title of the person you need to contact. If all you want to do is talk to the executive in charge of an initiative or a department, say so.

"Mary, my solution is utilized by the people in charge of the information technology departments inside my customers companies. Do you know who that would be?"

Yes, that would be Jack Smith.

In this example, notice how you still asked Mary for her opinion. You didn't say something like "I need to speak to the head of Information Technology." She probably wouldn't take that too well—after all, who are you to call her and use her as a rolodex? Instead, though, you politely and professionally told her what your solution was by telling her who already uses it and letting her decide if in fact she should make the connection for you.

Information Gathering

From this point on, Mary will be under the impression that the phone call is concluding. This is the time you can get a lot of additional information which can help you tremendously in your prospecting effort. The key to doing this is staying patient and polite.

I'll transfer you to Joe.

"Thank you. Would you happen to have Joe's extension?"

That would be 5678.

"So, if I'm dialing from the outside it would be 555 – 5678?"

No. Our internal exchange is 111. So it would be 111 – 5678.

Mary was ready to transfer you to Joe; but what if Joe isn't there? Asking for his information in this way allows you to dial directly to Joe's desk. Asking for his extension *first* is a non-threatening to way to frame the next request as to how to use that extension to dial in directly. Do *not* ask "Can I have his direct dial?" unless you want her to say *no* and hang up on you.

Cell Phone and Email

If you have gone this far, you may be able to pick up two additional access points for him. If Mary refuses to give this information to you thank her, tell her you understand and finish the call.

"You wouldn't have his cell-phone, would you?"

Yes, it's 123-4567

"Thank you so much; and before you transfer me, would he be receptive to receiving an introductory e-mail from me?"

Yes, probably. His e-mail address is name@thiscompany.com.

More Information

Do you want to be sure of his exact title? Delaying that request until now means you stand a better chance of getting the more valuable contact information *before* Mary's patience begins to ebb.

"Thank you. Would you have his exact title?"

Yes, that would be Chief Information Officer.

"Thank you so much Mary. Have a nice day."

Call Type 2: Speaking to Mr. Big

If you call enough eventually Mr. Big himself will pick up. To increase the chances of his being the one to pick up try calling early in the morning and late in the day. This is when he is at his desk trying to catch up on issues he couldn't get to during the day.

The Mr. Big Call

Mr. Big does not have any easy days. There are always problems that require his attention, expensive problems that a lot of very important people on his executive staff are not able to resolve without him. You could be calling Mr. Big as he has just lost a couple million dollars. But this is what he does and why he has the title of Mr. Big and its one of the things salespeople who call on Mr. Big need to be ready to deal with.

When Mr. Big doesn't know whom he is speaking to, he will be extremely brief. He's got important work to do. Expect no pleasantries to make you feel welcome, because if you need those he will know you're in the wrong place. Expect him to be tough and brief. He will use silence to allow you to expose yourself.

You will get one shot to tell him why you're calling.

Be deliberate and be tough yourself. You too can use silence; so don't be in a hurry to shoot your mouth off. You want to give the impression that you do this all the time and that you are used to speaking to someone in his position.

And relax. At some point, out of all the Mr. Bigs you speak to, you will inevitably make a mistake or stammer on something you've said a hundred times before. That's OK. It's all part of the game.

Expertly, rapidly guiding Mr. Big's mind to the point where he can really hear your ERS is key to making this a successful call and is what the following script is intended to do.

Mr. Big Answers

John Big.

"John, this is Kevin Leveille of Score Selling. I know you're not expecting my call, so I'll be brief."

There are a few items of importance in this tiny statement.

- ✓ Use his first name. Calling him "Mr. Lastname" shows formality and timidity and is proof you don't belong here.
- ✓ Tell him who you are and where you are from, so he knows he does not know you and isn't left to wonder.
- ✓ Telling him you know he is not expecting your call shows him you realize you are interrupting him.
- ✓ Telling him you will be brief will shows him he will not have to cut you off now.

Never

- Never ask him "How are you doing today?" Its social small talk and it will show you don't belong here. While it belongs in conversations with secretaries, it does not with Mr. Big.
- Never rush your words; speaking clearly gives him time to process your message.
- Never, ever say "I know you must be busy" or anything like that.

Deliver Your ERS

"My company provides solutions which can cut sales costs in half and still grow new business revenue from 200-400%. We do this by a combination of sales training, sales tools and automated sales management reporting. We did this for XYZ Corp who cut sales payroll costs by 55% and still grew new business acquisition by over 367% in less than six months."

"Can I get your permission to show an expert presentation to someone on your staff as to how we do this?"

The closing question is simple and non-threatening and gives Mr. Big plenty of room to agree to it.

- ✓ *Get your permission*: you recognize his authority.
- ✓ *Show an expert presentation*: an expert presentation tells him you are prepared to show expertise that he can get in a focused span of time.
- ✓ *Someone on your staff*: you are not requesting his personal time, though he may end up attending.

Mr. Big's Response

Mr. Big will answer your question with one of three possible responses.

1. Yes
2. No
3. Maybe

Really? Why?

Your answer to any of Mr. Big's responses is "Really? Why?"

Yes/No /Maybe.

"Really? Why yes / no / maybe?"

Example:

1. Mr. Big says "No." You respond with "Really? Why 'No?'"
2. Mr. Big says "Yes." You respond with "Really? Why 'Yes?'"
3. Mr. Big says "Maybe." You respond with "Really? Why 'Maybe?'"

This simple TWO QUESTION response works for any and all that Mr. Big would most likely say. As importantly, it draws him to give a bit more detail that you can work with.

Working with "No."

First off, if Mr. Big says "No" to this type of request, you may have qualified this account in a fraction of the time it would have taken you to call in at a lower level and chase someone there for an answer. That's good news.

But it is possible that Mr. Big has misunderstood what you do and what you are asking, so you can choose to clarify it.

No.

"Really? Why 'No?'"

Because, I just don't see how that is going to help us or We're not interested or We have something in place right now

"That's what I thought and that's exactly why I am calling, because many of my customers said the same thing and for good reason. After we met, some found we were a fit, others found we weren't, but all agreed it was a good use of their time. All I am looking to do is to give your company what I gave XYZ and ABC—an expert presentation—and leave it up to you."

"Now, I will be in New York next week; could I schedule some time with you or with someone on your staff?"

Why it works;

- ✓ "That's what I thought and that's exactly why I am calling because many of my customers said the same thing and for good reason…" you are taking Mr. Big off his position by affirming him in his perception; telling him he is wrong to see it the way he does won't work.
- ✓ "After we met, some found we were a fit, others found we weren't, but all agreed it was a good use of their time…" You lead him back to the reason for your call by showing it isn't about buying, it's about learning in a brief period of time.
- ✓ "All I am looking to do is to give your company what I gave ABC and XYZ—an expert presentation…" why should he deny his company what these others received?
- ✓ "and leave it up to you…" reaffirm that the way you do business is to leave it up to them to decide what is best for them.
- ✓ "Now, I will be in New York next week; could I schedule some time with you or with someone on your staff?" This appointment close brings your discussion to a logical conclusion. At this point, the issue should become one of timing and getting things scheduled.
- ✓ If Mr. Big repeats his "No," what else can you do? He is fully qualified out. Thank him, hang up and get to your next opportunity.

Dealing with "Maybe"

Dealing with "Maybe" is easier of course than with "No" though you will move to the same conclusion; closing for the meeting and by means of an almost identical approach.

Maybe.

"Really? Why 'Maybe?'"

Because we're finishing a major overhaul of that group right now or We're still trying to figure things out in that category or I am not sure you can really help us.

"That's what I thought and that's exactly why I am calling because many of my customers said the same thing and for good reason. After we met, some found we were a fit, others found we weren't, but all agreed it was a good use of their time. All I am looking to do is to give your company what I gave XYZ and ABC—an expert presentation—and leave it up to you."

"Now, I will be in Atlanta next week; could I schedule some time with you or with someone on your staff?"

You need to talk to Joe Sampson.

Dealing with "Yes."

"Yes" is great, however you still want to qualify why.

"Really? Why 'Yes?'"

Because we're in big trouble with that now or We've decided now is the time to work on that area of the business or I like what you're offering.

"I will be in New York next week; could I schedule some time with you or with someone on your staff?"

You need to talk to Joe Sampson.

Qualifying Mr. Big's Referral

When Mr. Big gives you the referral, you want to qualify that referral and get some additional information about him. You can accomplish this by staying firm and brief.

You need to talk to Joe Sampson.

"I'll do that. Why Joe?"

- *He's got some problems in that area…*
- *He's got some people that are developing a project along these lines now…*
- *He's been tasked with solving this problem for us…*

After each piece of information, ask;

- ✓ "Interesting. Why?" or
- ✓ "For example?" or
- ✓ "How do you mean that?"

Single Biggest Challenge

Summarize the line of questions with;

- ✓ "What do you see as Joe's single biggest challenge with respect to this?"

And let Mr. Big answer.

Qualify ROI

Test Mr. Big on budget.

- ✓ "Is a (your own true number) 20% reduction in (specific area) costs enough to justify a $100,000.00 investment this year?"
  - *Yes/ No / Maybe.*
  - "Really? Why 'Yes / No / Maybe?'"
  - *Because of…*

Or

- ✓ "If Joe came back to you to purchase a $100,000.00 solution for this, what kind of return on investment would you need?"
  - *300%*
  - "Really? Why 300%?"
  - *Because of…*

Keep the Door Open

This last question lets you call back to Mr. Big in the event that Joe doesn't cooperate with you.

"John thanks for your reference to Joe. I'll follow up with him. If for any reason he's not receptive or doesn't feel he's the right guy, will you take another call from me?"

Yes, but he is the right guy.

"Thanks, good-bye."

Call Type 3: the EIO Call

If Mr. Big has referred you to someone, you can be reasonably sure that he has charged this person with an initiative that you can help with. Mr. Big may in fact be using this call you made to him as the means by which he tasks this individual with an improvement; your contact in that case becomes the Executive Initiative Owner.

Speaking to the Executive Initiative Owner

The Executive Initiative Owner is the guy who owns your decision. He is the one that has been directed by someone with Executive authority to head up an Initiative--or project--to change something at the company. He could very likely become your Campaigner. He is the one that is going to field 90% of your communications with that company. Here's how you engage him.

Mr. Big Referral

If you received a referral from Mr. Big, leave him a voicemail message.

"Hi Joe this is Kevin Leveille of Score Selling. I just had a conversation with John Big about (your solution and the way you are able to save money.) He suggested I meet with you.

Feel free to give me a call at (phone number) or e-mail me at (the e-mail address.) Thank you."

Nine times out of ten that guy is going to call you back.

Speaking with the EIO

"Hi Joe this is Kevin Leveille of Score Selling. I know you're not expecting my call, so I'll be brief. I spoke to John Big about what my company does (insert your Executive Reference Statement.) He suggested I speak with you to set a meeting. I will be in Atlanta the week after next, would that work for you?"

Once you have the meeting scheduled, you can ask for some additional information.

"When I spoke to him, John (Mr. Big) seemed to think that "X" issue was important. Do you know why that might be…?"

Yes, because of…

Setting the meeting with the EIO should not be challenging if you have approached him through Mr. Big.

Conclusion: Alternate Approach to the EIO

If you are contacting the EIO directly, simply adapt your approach that you used on Mr. Big.

Chapter 12: Voicemail Campaigns

What is the Voicemail Campaign?

A Voicemail Campaign is a series of five or six related voicemail messages that increase the chances of making a connection with the prospect either by getting him to answer his phone when you call or by prompting him to return your call.

Why Voicemail Fails

Salespeople hate voicemail. It is universally seen as a nuisance. Salespeople think of voicemail as a wall between them and the prospect. When a salesperson makes a call, if he gets voicemail he treats it as a missed opportunity, often not even leaving a voicemail.

When salespeople do leave voicemail, they only leave one or two at the most, because they do not want the prospect getting mad at them for being too persistent. They use a one-size fits all message if they have one at all. Salespeople's average voicemail sounds something like;

"Hi this is Don Johnson calling from XYZ Corp. We provide services in the areas of IT outsourcing, business continuance and backup and recovery. I am just trying to get in touch with you to see about your needs. Please give me a call when you can. I am at 555-5555. Thanks."

When they cannot get through to an important prospect they report to their sales manager that they "left him a message," shrugging as if to say "Well, what else can I do—he won't call me back?"

Voicemail is Mission Critical

Yet the prospect views his voicemail as a mission critical application.

Prospects Listen to Voicemail

In the case of your voice mail, you need to know that your prospect will listen to it. You see, even the most hard-nosed prospect tends to listen to the entire sales message, because he wants to make sure that he doesn't hear something like "call me back when you can because Mr. Jones--your CEO--said to call you." That is a confirmed fact.

It's also the reason why your prospect *hates* most sales voicemail. Contrary to what most salespeople fear, the prospect does actually listen to salespeople's voicemail. And for the most part he can't stand what he hears.

Educating the Prospect

Voicemail educates the prospect. While your prospecting effort is a continual request for the prospect to learn about you, it is also a continual education to your prospect as to who you already are; your tone, your message, the content, whether you are well spoken; all of these register with your prospect.

Voicemail educates the prospect, most of the time about things you wish he wasn't learning.

Like Radio Advertising

Businesses pay thousands and thousands of dollars for radio advertising for a fifteen to thirty second spot to highlight their product or service. During these few seconds, they hope that their prospect is in a car somewhere and that their prospect might be paying attention. Yet you can leave a targeted message for your specific prospect and do it for free.

Why You Need Good Voicemail

Create an Impression

You need to impress your prospect. You need to stand out from the competition. You need to improve the results from your prospecting efforts. You need to get return calls. So you need good voicemail.

Persistence

You have got to be persistent today and that means making repeat calls on the same prospect until you can get a pickup. Good voicemail allows you to make those repeat calls because good voicemail educates the prospect that you are the type of professional he should be speaking to.

Sample Voicemail Campaign

The following Voicemail Campaign will allow you to leave 5 voicemails in a row for the prospect. They link together so well that if your prospect was on vacation and came back to find only your five voicemails he would not only NOT be upset, he would be looking forward to speaking with you.

How Often

How often should you leave these messages? That depends on you and your industry. Some leave messages every day for prospects; others like to leave one per week. Find your own preference, but stick to the campaign.

Executive Reference Statement

When calling your prospect you need to have something good to say. The Executive Reference Statement will help you do that.

This is exactly what you did for the Calling High section. You will just create more of them for your voicemail campaign.

Executive Reference Statement

The Executive Reference Statement, or ERS, is the mini-commercial for your solution. The ERS will address your prospect's hot points as they relate to your solution's benefits.

What are your prospect's hot points? Safe bets include;

- ✓ Business Improvement—growth, profit
- ✓ Competitiveness, survival
- ✓ Cost Reduction

You can hit your prospect's hot points by focusing on big picture business issues and not on features of your solution. Do not be overly technical in describing features and capabilities of your solution. You could lose his interest fast. Instead focus on the business gains that your solution provides to your customers.

Your ERS could run as follows;

- ✓ "We provide solutions which…"

- Lower costs OR increase profitability OR increase revenue
    - By how much %
- ✓ "We do this by…"
    - Automating OR eliminating OR improving OR enabling *something*
- ✓ "We've done this for companies like…"
    - ABC and XYZ.
- ✓ "I am calling to…"
    - Set an appointment with you to discuss…

Sample ERS

"My company provides solutions which can cut sales costs in half and still grow new business revenue from 200-400%. We do this by a combination of sales training, sales tools and automated sales management reporting. We did this for XYZ Corp who cut sales payroll costs by 55% and still grew new business acquisition by over 367% in less than six months."

Create Three to Four Versions of Your ERS

You need to create three to four versions of your ERS so your voicemails do not sound like the same thing. You can accomplish this fairly easily by using 3-4 different customer stories.

Voicemail 1: The Introduction

"Hi John, this is Bill Smith from ABC Company. I'm calling you to provide some information about what my company does and how we might be able to help. Now, you don't know me, but feel free to call me back if something here resonates with you. What my company does is;"

- ✓ Executive Reference Statement One.

"Thank you. My contact information is as follows."

Note that the Introduction Voicemail is very simple and brief. Let the prospect know who you are, what you do and how to get in touch with you. The special stuff here is in the "You don't know me" statement. This is an example of carrying on a live conversation through your message. Most voicemail sounds like a recording of someone talking to the machine, right? But when you can make a statement of fact in your voicemail which when the prospect listens to it, it speaks to him at that moment; you are leaving messages which can carry on a live conversation.

This has an impact on the prospect, partly because you save him the time of wondering if he does know you, but mostly because you have the guts to do away with any pretense. He probably won't return your call at this point, but he will remember you.

Voicemail 2: Professionally Persistent

"Hi John, this is Bill Smith from ABC Company. I'd like to see if there's a basis for providing some information that might be helpful to you. What my company does is;"

- ✓ Executive Reference Statement Two.

"Now, it'd be nice, but I don't expect you to call me back right away. However, this is an important call for me, so if it's all right, I'd like to be professionally persistent and try you again. If that's not OK please let me know."

This voicemail will stand out in your prospects mind.

And for salespeople this voicemail continues the live conversation; you show him you do not expect a call back! How often does he hear that? But you say it in such a way that it makes sense, which is as important. You "get it."

You tell him he is an important prospect; another sign, in his mind, that you "Get it."

Additionally, you have received permission to continue calling! It is a professional responsibility for you and who can argue that? And since you continue to add value by telling him great things in your ERS your chances of a call back are growing.

And given him an opt-out! One of the most important items to include in email communications just made its way to voicemail thanks to the solid professional you are. Sure, most salespeople view this as a gimmick to get the guy to call back. While the prospect doesn't view it that way, he is nonetheless given an incentive to call you back.

Getting him on the phone after this means you have a prospect that not only knows you, but respects you.

Voicemail 3: I Know You

"Hi John, this is Bill Smith from ABC Company. I know you cannot return every call like this that comes to you, so I wanted to keep the initiative and let you know more about my firm."

- ✓ Executive Reference Statement Three.

"Thank you. My contact information is as follows."

His first reaction when he receives this message may be amusement as he thinks "Him again? I wonder what he's got for me this time?" The live conversation continues when you let him know that *you* know he cannot return every call and you wanted to keep the initiative.

Now he is going to begin to feel like he is giving you--a good salesperson--the idea that he doesn't want to talk to you. He will begin to feel a little bad about that, but then your message takes that away from him as you show him how that it's understandable. And he actually begins to feel good.

If he doesn't return your call by now, he is either not a prospect, is a horrible time manager (common) or is so busy he simply *cannot* get back to you. But you're not done.

Voicemail 4: Busy Guy

"Hi John, this is Bill Smith from ABC Company. I know there's 10,000 things on your to do list, and I am probably not at the top of it, but if something here makes sense to you, I'd love to hear from you."

- ✓ Executive Reference Statement four.

"Thank you. My contact information is as follows."

You are helping this prospect save considerable face about his inability to give you a call back. That is so important, because when he does pick up he is going to feel very different about you than he would someone who left a bunch of "call me back" voicemails.

Voicemail 5: Good Bye

"Hi John, this is Bill Smith from ABC Company."

"I realize that right now is too rough a time for your schedule to fit me in and I fully understand. I just want to thank you for your patience in receiving my messages and I hope to provide some helpful information to you at some later time. I hope it's all right if I follow up with you in the near future."

"Thank you. My contact information is as follows."

This prospect is either not a prospect for your solution at all or he is physically unable to get back to you. If he does not call you back you are free to repeat this easy process in the future. Like, maybe next month.

Moving Really Stuck Accounts

Use this next voicemail at your own discretion. You should only use it when you feel there is clearly an indication that your prospect could be ill. It is used when Mr. Big referred you to this contact and you need to call Mr. Big back to be sure you have the right guy, but don't want to upset the contact by going back over his head, even if he won't return your call.

"Hi John--I haven't heard from you and however unlikely it is, I just want to rule out that you're not suffering personal loss or illness. Please forgive me if I am misinterpreting this, but I have a strange feeling about this that I don't want to ignore it. I will be checking in with Jim to verify your condition. Obviously, if it's nothing serious, I will understand and move on. But feel free to let me know if I have misunderstood in the meantime."

NEVER Say

These "Nevers" go for all voicemails.

- Just trying to reach you about…
- I know you're busy...
- Call me back / Return my call
- It's me again
- I left you a message the other day
- or sent you an email or wrote you a letter)
- I am calling back
- You didn't call me back
- Uh...um

- I'd like to meet with you about…
- I'd really appreciate a callback

Conclusion

Switch up your call times. Try early in the morning then late in the afternoon. Try in the middle of the day. Call a couple times in one day. Wait a day or two then try again. Keep calling. Prospects today don't mind, just as long as you don't sound like a broken record. Usually, your prospect will have either called you back or would have answered the phone prior to leaving the fifth voice mail. On the other hand, you may find that as time goes on it takes five messages to get executives to give you a call back.

Chapter 13: **Effective Email**

Email

One of the most powerful, versatile tools since the telephone has come online with universal acceptance in the Information Age; Email.

Yet many salespeople do not understand its power to make an impression or to kill one. We'll cover some of the basic elements of email introductions; what to do, when to do it and how to use it, including one astoundingly simple yet amazingly effective way to impact your prospect with email.

Sales Email

The great thing about sales email is that you have perfect content control over the message. Unlike a phone call you do not have to worry about flubbing your message or the pitch of your voice or forgetting what you wanted to say. Email can be crafted perfectly before sending it out.

Also, the prospect tends to prefer email communications as a rule. He can speed-read it, it isn't considered interruptive—at least not like a phone call and it's real easy for him to respond to.

Email can be a softer initial communication if it is done correctly and can also be used effectively once inside the sales cycle with the customer. Inside the sales cycle, email can be used to keep contact and to get back in if you find yourself marginalized by the prospect.

It is easier to see if your prospect is considering your message. If you need to maintain some kind of written transcript of your communications or even get a read receipt for email that you've sent, you can do that, too.

Email Guidelines

All the foregoing information about the effectiveness of email as a sales tool still goes so long as you keep in mind the rules around email.

No Spam

Any unsolicited email is spam, plain and simple. You will be sending email to the prospect under this program but you will most often be doing that upon request or permission or at the very least after having received a referral.

Fast Formality

Email is fast formality—it is not informal. Addressing your prospect professionally and considerately at all times is important.

Brief

Email should be brief. Two to five sentences at most. Prospects do not want to receive a run on letter in the form of email. It simply won't get read. Focus on one idea and keep it inside 1-3 paragraphs.

Plain Text

Nothing so says you don't get it than to be inserting some fancy stationary or formatting in email. Corporate email servers mangle even unformatted text sometimes. And you should keep any messages you send to less than 72 characters per line, so you won't end up with a hacked look on other side of the Exchange® server.

Never

Never send anything you wouldn't want to have end up on the front page of the New York Times; not only is email easy to forward and send anywhere, there can also be legal issues which may make it easy to do so.

Always

Pause before sending any important email.

Nine Email Types

The following emails can be used in different parts of your sales process.

Pre-Email

Send the Pre-Email to improve the likelihood of pick-ups when you are making prospecting phone calls.

> "Hi Joe;
> I hope you've been well. I just wanted to let you know I will be calling you in the next day or so to see about our discussion. Feel free to let me know if that's ok; I look forward to speaking."

Customer Re-connect

"I hope you're well. I wanted to let you know I will be placing a call to you Tuesday morning to see if you might be willing to have lunch with me sometime over the next week or two. Just to say thank you for the business you've done with me and to see if there might be some ways I can improve for you. Feel free to let me know if that might work when I call. I look forward to speaking with you."

The Permission Request

I got an email from someone I didn't know the other day--you know, SPAM!

Well, actually it wasn't spam, but by the time I figured out what it was doing in my box, it should have been.

Don't let this happen to you!

When you are prospecting executives and you get someone that's told you that you need to email Joe So&So over in finance, DO NOT FIRE OFF YOUR BLATHERING sales junk. Take a moment and introduce your BSJ with the following introductory email.

Set the Subject to a something like; "Permission per Sally's Reference."

In the body, say something like;

"I've got some information I'd like to send to you--it concerns improving performance or reducing costs or a customer story. If you don't want to receive it, let me know. I will hold on to it for a later time."

"I'll be sending it out (2 days from now) on Wednesday."

Thanks, your name.

KEEP IT BRIEF!

He needs to be able to scan it quickly and decide--very likely--to accept it. Rather, it seems OK to NOT take you up on your offer to reject it.

Three important things happen when you do this.

First, you haven't violated his space by invading it with something that is likely to be deemed spam. You have subtly impressed upon the prospect that you get it; you think like he does. You have shown him that you are an advocate and want to protect him and his precious time from being occupied with affairs that he knows are not a good use of his time.

Second, you haven't told him he's going to need to take action in order to receive your e-mail. So you're not trying to get him to do anything.

Third, you've put a psychological seed in his mind so that the chances of your follow up e-mail being rejected as unfamiliar and invasive should be dramatically reduced.

I took this approach a couple years ago when I had received an email list of 100 CEO's of a very tough market segment I wanted to get access to. When I sent out the introductory note, I received eight (8) "Don't send" replies. Saved me the time of calling on these and told me that the other 92 were now receptive to my information.

The Introductory Email

Your introductory email is that note you send after you've talked with the prospect by phone. The inevitable question comes "Can you send me some information?"

At this time more than half of all salespeople howl, resist, press for an appointment or bail completely.

The other half goes off and begins a two-hour effort to create the marketing package they are going to send. Two days later that marketing package, so carefully crafted, is deposited, not so carefully, in the prospects waste bin.

Ouch!

Been there done that?

Let's take a different tack. Since 99% of the interested prospects we talk to are going to want to receive something from us why don't we take a moment and be ready for that event?

Format of the Introductory Email

The format of the introductory email is simple; whatever you think gets your point across. If you want help, a useful format follows.

Start with information about who you are, then what you do, followed by why you're different and what that means to your customers. Finish with why they should give you an opportunity to talk further with them. Refer to your Elevator Message content to help you get moving quickly.

Who We Are

List some bullet points about who you are. Avoid the "Take it or Leave it" message statements like "We're an Asphalt Paver." Draw some color and impact with statements like "We're an Information Age Human Resources Company with Guaranteed Results."

What We Do

Tell them something about the type of service you provide. Describe your service in terms of the benefits that you bring to your customers.

Why We're Better

Pick a couple items that only your company provides. Make sure they're the best features of your solution. For instance, you might say things like "There are two things which separate us from our competitors..."

One of the keys to doing this is to select a Strategic Attribute. Strategic attributes are those qualities that your customer is always saying he wants, but which are difficult to ascertain. Things like service, response, expertise, stability, and reliability.

For instance, if financial strength is an issue in a tempestuous market, and if your customers are sensitive to the ability of their provider to be around for years to come, you'll want to pull a Fact that supports that statement.

Facts are completely obvious and readily verifiable. Things like the age of your company, the size, and the location. Consider, for instance the size of your company. If you were the largest organization in your market, you might mention that as a verifiable supporting statement to your Strategic Value.

Can you see the obvious difference between these two statements?

- ✓ "We have the most financially stable company in the industry."
- ✓ "Due to our market leading size and financial strength, we are able to provide our customers with the assurance of having the most financially stable company on their side."

What Our Customers Say

Insert a customer reference or two and the great benefit they have achieved. If you have percentages or financial savings, etc., USE THEM.

Why You Should Consider Us

You have great service and support and you will be there and continue to help them to excel in the area of consideration, etc.

When you send an introductory email like this you will dramatically, positively and immediately impact your prospecting effort.

Sample Introductory Email

- HRT is an Information-Age Human Resources Training Company (see www.yourcompanysite.com.) We are the sole authorized trainers of the HRT Solution. Our mission is to equip the motivated HR professional with the tools and methods to survive this new Age of Information.
- We solve HR and HR management problems like not being able to get to enough qualified candidates, training of current employees and outsourcing.
- These have always been problems for HR Professionals; only now these old problems have got new causes. The Information Age has brought a totally new prospect for today's HR Professional to deal with (for more go here.)
- Why HRT training? Because everything else is too old (see here.)

  - Visit www.yourcompanysite.com for more details about how to prepare. And be sure to sign up for the newsletter while you're there.
  - Best Regards.

Networking Follow Up

Use this as follow up to a chance meeting, or a networking follow up. Also when you unintentionally backburner someone for a period of time and now want to re-establish contact.

This type of simple follow up is for anyone from just above a cold contact to someone you know but just haven't connected with in some time.

Your goal is to get permission, implied or otherwise, to communicate with them. Secondly, you want them to recognize your subsequent emails when you do send them out and not ditch them as spam.

Anchor Reference

This is where you draw a point of common reference; like where you met or last talked. Be specific--this is email, so it doesn't need to be--nor should it be--drawn out.

"I met you at (be specific)…we spoke about…"

Inform

Let them know what it is you're connecting with them about. Do you want them to receive or look out for some additional communication you'll be forwarding? Be specific.

"I wanted to let you know that I will be sending you an update on [insert relevant news topic.]"

Or,

"…sending you an occasional update on relevant developments at my company."

Right to Refuse

It doesn't get any more important than letting them know that you understand their right to refuse your communication. This is the de facto protocol of email marketing.

"Feel free to let me know if that's not ok; or if you have any questions."

Close simply and warmly.

"Thanks."

Request for Follow Up

When: After a cold call conversation etc.

Inform

"Wanted to let you know that I will be sending you an update on [insert relevant news topic.]"

Or

"…sending you an occasional update on relevant developments at my company."

"Feel free to let me know if that's not ok or if you have any questions. Thanks."

Sample

"Thanks for taking a moment for my call. I enjoyed speaking with you about your interests as well as your business."

"I just wanted to let you know I will be sending you an occasional update on my company. I hope that's OK—if not, feel free to let me know."

"I look forward to talking with you again, soon."

Regards, Your name.

After Sending Information

Use this when you send anything to a prospect that you intend to follow up on.

"Enclosed is my proposal. Thank you for taking some time to review it and to speak with me by phone. I will stand by should you have any questions or concerns and I look forward to being in touch soon."

Email Hovering

Ever set an appointment, with all the right prospecting efforts behind it, only to receive an email requesting the date to be changed? Ever notice that this is one of the sure signs that things are about to derail in your account?

Why is that?

Three reasons

First, something has happened on the prospect's side. That much is clear, since, by definition, they need to reschedule the meeting.

You don't really know what it is, how serious it is, or if it is serious at all. But they have made the decision to move you. As SINCERE as they may have been in setting the appointment and as real as they may be now in the resetting of the appointment, they are moving you out.

That is NOT possible without a corresponding DECREASE in the enthusiasm they had for meeting with you in the first place. It's a fact.

Second, there is administrative bother. Now any attempts you begin to make to KEEP the appointment, to reschedule it, are going to be an administrative bother for the prospect. He has to check his email, then check his calendar, then check with the other people's calendar, then back with you.

That's one repetition of that event and if he has to repeat it that's even more of a problem. Remember, his enthusiasm has already waned. And this is coupled with the fact that he is dealing with you in cyberspace.

Third, they are dealing with an unreal you. You are distant, unreal, and unpersuasive and it is far easier now to dismiss you by typing a few words out and being done with the whole business.

So, what do you do?

Get out of email!

Get back on the phone and reestablish person-to-person contact. This is the most tenuous place you can be; you need to realize that once you are in "Hover" mode, you are more likely than ever to be shut out for good.

Send an immediate reply requesting they take your call. Something like "May I call you to avoid playing tag email?"

Something that simple will reduce your chances of being bottled off to email oblivion.

Emails for Appointment Setting

Use these emails to be thorough when setting appointments.

Immediately After Scheduling a Meeting

"Thanks for taking the time for my call; I look forward to meeting with you Tuesday September 16 at 3:00 PM at your office. I will be prepared to discuss _______ and I look forward to the opportunity to learn more about _____. In the meantime, should you have any questions feel free to let me know."

Sending an Outlook® Meeting Request does NOT replace the above.

Confirming a Meeting Just Prior to Showing Up

"I look forward to meeting with you tomorrow at 3 PM to talk about ____ and to hear more about ______. Feel free to contact me with any questions in the meantime."

Follow Up Immediately After a Meeting

"Thanks for taking the time to meet with me today; I enjoyed hearing about your company and I look forward to meeting again. I will be getting the questions / issues regarding ______ addressed and will follow up with you by ______ . In the meantime, feel free to let me know if you have any questions for me. Thanks again."

Persistent Email

Use these emails to persistently approach difficult to reach prospects.

Errors

"We've had email (or phone) problems in case you called and couldn't get through; I'll try again later; if that doesn't work, please let me know. Thanks."

Haven't Heard

"Have not heard from you and I am assuming that is due to your workload and not due to any change in our plans to work together. I will be sending out some additional ideas to you this afternoon and will be in touch."

Persistent Mega-Follow Up

Use this email when you've been trying for some time to get in touch with the prospect.

- ✓ I hope you are well.
- ✓ I am sure things are extremely busy on your side of things; I wish you the best in your efforts.
- ✓ I know that in today's business environment, it is not easy to feel interested or enthusiastic about every call you might get from an entity--such as my firm--which is unknown to you."
- ✓ I hope that the introductory information I have provided may soften this a bit and provide us an opportunity to connect at a time that is convenient for you.
- ✓ With that in mind, I will be attempting to get in touch with you this week;
- ✓ I trust that's OK.

During Sales Cycle

Use this email campaign when your sales cycle looks like it might be close to hitting a snag. This approach uses a variation of the messaging utilized in the voicemail campaign.

Email #1

"Sam,

"Feel free to let me know if you have any advice for me. I spoke with Jim yesterday and he was kind enough to suggest there may be some value in re-submitting my proposal with other options. Do you have any advice or suggestions that you could offer? I'd appreciate any feedback you could provide. Thanks for your consideration."

Email #2

"Sam;

"I wanted to take a moment to thank you for your time the other week and to say I am excited by the prospect of continuing the relationship with ______. In that regard, I have posted a summary document for download at http://_______ that I believe you will find interesting. You can access it using ______as username and password of _____(case sensitive); so for you that's obviously _____ and _____. I will follow up to ensure your receipt, if that's ok."

Email #3

"Sam;

"Thanks for receiving my email information last week regarding my current proposal to ____. I know you must be attending to a heavy workload, so I thought I would reach out to you and see if you might be able to offer me any advice. You are an important client to me, so if the next few days don't work for you, I hope you don't mind if I remain professionally persistent and reach out again sometime. Thanks for your consideration and have a blessed day.

PS. The information I sent out last week is posted at www._____ (so it doesn't get stuck in a spam filter) username and pw is ___ & ___."

Emails that Deal with Resistance

Incumbent Competitor

Here's a whopper to use when your prospect is in love with your competitor and his incumbent.

"I understand your commitment to the XYZ Company and it sounds like they are taking care of you; if you were my customer I would certainly work hard to do the same. Many of my customers felt the same way about their provider when I initially contacted them and while not all of them became customers, all of them found that they got some benefit from our meeting.

For those eventually who did become our customer--companies like ____ and _____--it was because they found clear and compelling advantages over anything available in the market today. If you don't find the same advantages, you're better off not changing. However, you should know what those advantages are; that's why I am contacting you.

For now all I am looking to do is meet and share that information with you and to leave it with you in the event you have a future need for our help. I will be in touch with you to see about arranging a time to meet. Feel free to let me know if you have any questions for me in the meantime, or if you'd like to suggest a time. Thanks and Best Regards."

Service Problems

Clear this with your legal department before using it—be careful not to implicate yourself or your company.

Having said this, this email can be used to crack open a door that has been slammed shut due to a service failure. Adapt it for use.

- ✓ "I completely understand if you do not feel enthusiastic at the prospect of hearing from me or my company. One of the hallmarks of good business is learning from the past; we certainly try to learn from ours. The experience we have had with ______ has provided us ample opportunity to learn. And we have learned.
- ✓ "My sole reason for contacting you is to convey this to you and to willingly listen to any concerns or advice you would like to share with me."
- ✓ "Please be assured I would not dream of attempting to ask you to revisit your decision until this fact is credibly communicated with you. Again, I am asking for a chance to do that in person."
- ✓ "I humbly request your patience with my efforts to arrange this meeting, as I intend to be professionally persistent in doing so. I will attempt to contact you this week and will be standing by at [cell phone] if you choose to call."
- ✓ "In the meantime, feel free to let me know your thoughts or preferences; I will treat any reply with the highest priority. Thank you for your kind consideration."

Conclusion

Email is a great medium for selling; but always be very sure to keep your email communications—and all your sales communications—within the parameters of the law, your company's human resources policy and good taste.

Chapter 14: **Streaming and Blending Your Messages**

What is Streaming and Blending?

Streaming and Blending is about mixing the mediums of your sales communications and delivering them in a logical schedule to the prospect.

Rather than pour all your energies into one medium—such as phone—you blend phone with email, letters and voicemail to have a maximum impact on the prospect.

OPEN GATE™

What is OPEN GATE™?

OPEN GATE™ is an eight step prospecting and follow up process that centers on the mailing or emailing of a newsletter. Specifically;

1. Objective: the planning step for the remaining seven steps.
2. Phone: the call that kicks off the campaign.
3. Email: the email that reaffirms the call.

4. Newsletter: the newsletter that is either emailed or mailed.
5. Gratitude: the immediate follow up to the newsletter.
6. Ask: the request for information.
7. Talk: the conversation with the prospect.
8. Enter: the invitation to meet.

Information

The key to the success for OPEN GATE™ is the Newsletter. The Newsletter is the awesome piece of information that you offer to your prospects to draw them in to experience your site, more of your information, your company and your solution. Let's consider the individual stages of the OPEN GATE™ prospecting solution.

Objective: Day 1

Decide what you want to accomplish and what it is you are going to send. This is the Objective step. Plan out the seven steps of the campaign and pay special attention to the quality of the newsletter you will send out. Since the OPEN GATE™ Newsletter is so important to the campaign; you need to know more about what it should look like.

Sample Features of an OPEN GATE™ Newsletter

Remember it is all about information. Information is vital; the more crucial the better—a brochure about sales nonsense is going to educate the prospect about how worthless the information you've got to give him really is. Instead, a Newsletter should inform them of something they need to know. Again, visualize what you are sending them as something they have bought and paid for; that is the level of quality of information that you'll need to consistently deliver.

Make sure that your title statement is attention getting. Keys to writing a gripping title include the following; ask a question, describe a problem and be specific. An example might be "Are These Three Problems Holding You Back from More Sales?" Ineffective titles include meaningless benefit statements 'Prospecting Solutions for Sales Professionals.'

Once you have finished preparing your Newsletter, you are ready to let your prospect know about it.

Space the delivery of each of these communications by anywhere from two to five days from when the prospect receives it, not when you send it. For instance if you call someone on day one referencing something you don't put in the mail for another five days, you'll be anywhere from seven to ten days before it's in their hands. In that instance you should call them the date that you are putting the Newsletter in the mail. That will keep the flow of your communications consistent and avoid the prospect wondering where this communication came from which appeared "out of the blue." Missing the timing of each of these segments could mean the failure of your entire campaign. Use a planner so that it is always with you and can alert you when it is time to sit down and call or e-mail.

Phone: Day 2

Let them know its coming. Give them a phone call and either leave them a message or tell them it's on its way. A sample voicemail might be;

"Joe, just a courtesy call; wanted to let you know I'm sending you a [prime title]; it may be of special interest to you because in it is [highlight title] which might be beneficial [in this way.] No need for you to return the call unless you want to; but I am at 555-1212."

Sample

"Hi Joe, this is just a courtesy call; I want to let you know I'm sending you a complimentary white paper titled "Are These Seven Problems Killing Your Prospecting Efforts?" It may be of special interest to you if you ever had a key prospect that will not let you in or wondered why you can't get all the leads that you would like to have. There's an explanation and solution to each. No need for you to return the call unless you want to. This is Kevin Leveille and I'm at (770) 555-5555; or email Kevin@scoreselling.com"

Email: Day 5

The next step is to offer a second, more visible advertisement of the quality of the information that's coming. This time, send an email note that advises them of what is coming. Something like;

"Joe; [tantalizingly cool title of Newsletter] will be on its way to you [by date.] It may offer something of interest if you ever had to [address this problem which {highlight title} solves, or that key problem which {highlight title 2} solves. No need to reply unless you don't want it; thanks for letting me send it to you."

Sample.

"Joe, my free white paper titled "Are These Seven Problems Killing Your Prospecting Efforts" will be on its way to you by the seventeenth of this month. It might be of interest if your sales deals have ever been stalled by a prospect's voicemail, or if you have ever run into the voicemail problem when prospecting. There is a section devoted to voicemail messages that actually gets your prospects to call you back. No need to reply unless you don't want it; thanks."

Best Regards,
Kevin Leveille
Kevin@scoreselling.com.

Newsletter Arrives: Day 7

Deliver the Newsletter itself. By now, when your piece arrives, they'll be expecting it. Even, if you've done your job well, anticipating it. Of course, they might not elbow their CEO out of the way in order to get their hands on it, but you can rest assured they will know it when they see it. As opposed to all the other prospecting efforts you made in the past that ended up deleted or trashed.

For special prospects--say your top ten or twenty--if you send an email, you can also provide a hard copy via postage mail a day or two after the original Newsletter would be received. If you sent a hard copy, provide an email version. This gives you two chances to make the impression and ensures that your prospect has received it.

MAKE SURE IT"S A VALUABLE PIECE! (Did I mention that yet?) Keep in mind, you've done all this work now and your prospect is expecting to receive something of value. Do not let them down, or you will be in a worse place than you would be if you never let them know it was coming. NO SALES LITERATURE!!

Gratitude: Day 9

Send an email thanking the prospect for receiving the information. Ask for feedback. Say something like;

- ✓ "Joe; Thanks for being part of a small circle of business people who let us keep them informed. I hope the [insert information title] I sent was helpful in some way. I'm always trying to make it better so your feedback is precious to me. Please feel free to share any advice you've got and I'll do what I can to improve. Thanks again."

An e-mail is better than anything else you could provide at this point. That's the easiest thing to reply to. If you send a letter or a handwritten note he cannot reply directly to it and that will tend to discourage feedback. And certainly don't expect him to pick up the phone and call you. A good rule of thumb would be that you don't expect him to take any initiative at all. Make it easy for him.

Ask: Day 10

Get back on the phone and call. Your goal here is to ask his opinion; nothing more. You're going to see how proceeding in this direction will allow your qualified prospects to identify themselves.

There are two different paths to concluding the call, based on whether or not you get him on the phone when you call or whether you need to leave voicemail.

Voicemail Sample

If you get voicemail, leave a message as to why you are calling. I like to keep it brief here.

- ✓ "Hi Joe. I am just making a call to ask you a quick question; I'm looking for ideas for the next newsletter and I always like to have input from people like you when I can get it. Not urgent, but if you can help me, I'd really appreciate it. I will/will not try you back. [Leave phone number] Thanks."

Talk: Day 11+

The conversation that happens once you get him on the phone.

Your goal in carrying out this call is two-fold. First you want to see if there is an interest in getting together with you to begin a sales campaign. Second, you want to know what problems are out there and what your prospects want to receive in the form of information from you. Because, if they tell you what they want, and you give it to them you have just vaulted over every other sales person that they have ever dealt with. You have not even asked for permission to sell them something yet. You are dealing with that prospect according to his protocols and he is going to be very comfortable with you because you have demonstrated to him that you 'get it.'

If you keep to the program, you can't go wrong. Because if he does not have any problems which your solution will solve for him at this time, you have just found that out in a very low key, value-added, comfortable way for the prospect. He will be glad to take your call at a later time and certainly may even call you when he has a need. A need that he recognizes, thanks to your consistent delivery of information that is designed to help identify that problem.

Conversation Sample

"Hi Joe. I'm calling a few folks to get their take on the [prime piece.] Would you be able to help me?"

Sure.

"Did you review it? Do you have any suggestions as to how I can improve it?"

Positive Response

No, I think you're doing great. I enjoyed the last piece.

"What resonated with you?"

Well, the part about….

"What would it have in it next time, if it was something you couldn't wait to open?"

'Plane tickets to Hawaii-- har dee har!

"Yeah; I'll see what I can do...but, seriously, other than that, any information business-wise—I'd really appreciate any ideas."

No, not really.

"Regarding [what you do] what's one of the problems you'd like to make go away?"

Well, it would be great if I no longer had to deal with problem-name…

Repeat what he said as a question;

"It would be great if you no longer had to deal with problem-name?"

Yes.

"Why?"

Because of….

Continue to expand on the issue until you are fully educated as to the problem he is having. Ask;

"Why...and how does that happen...?"

Close for the appointment, when it's time

"Well, Joe, I appreciate what you've shared. Let me ask you a question--if I had some information which could help you, do you want to wait for the newsletter version of it, or would you prefer we meet and take a closer look at it?"

Let's meet. [Move to **Entry** step.]

Or, he says;

Let's wait.

"No problem, thanks for your time."

Negative Response

Let's rewind and assume your prospect gave you a negative response to your question.

"Hi Joe. I'm calling a few folks to get their take on the [prime piece.] Would you be able to help me?"

Sure.

"Did you review it? Do you have any suggestions as to how I can improve it?"

No--nothing applied.

"When you say nothing really applies, HOW do you mean that?"

Well, nothing applied what more can I say about it?

"I'm sorry this wasn't a good use of your time, I really hate it that I've used your time and not added any value to you. Would you be able to help me?"

I'll try.

"How could I have done better? What would you have included in there that wasn't?"

Oh, well, recruiting is a big deal.

"Really? Why?"

Well because…

Continue the discussion until you can ask for the appointment.

Entry Step

At this point, you've got the appointment to come in. Now what you want to do is to set up a pre-meeting conference call to prepare for that meeting.

Make sure that you have scheduled a date and time for the meeting BEFORE you ask for the pre-conference call. This will keep your prospect focused and be less likely to cause a scheduling mishap later. It also keeps you focused on one item at a time.

Sample

"Now, before I go, would you give me a minute or two in order to make the information I am going to present the best that I can? I don't want to talk in deep generalities when we meet, but tailor it to you. Does that sound OK?"

Sure.

"Would you take a phone call from me next week to talk about some of those items and allow me to incorporate them before I show up? Takes about 7-11 minutes."

Objections

Are limited—he's just given you the appointment.

Usually—*why don't we do it now?* In which case you say, "OK."

Sometimes, they might ask;

Another call to get ready? How complex is this going to be?

In which case you simply answer;

"I'm going to deliver a presentation titled [insert title.] I'd really like to make it even more relevant by tailoring it to you. Don't you think?"

OK. When you want to do it?

Set the appointment for the call.

Problems and Objections

There are not a lot of objections that come up here, because what you're doing is so non-threatening that the prospect is not likely to offer a lot of resistance. You're giving him a choice as to whether or not to meet with you. You're also giving him a choice as to whether not to set up a pre conference call meeting. But if he does have an objection, usually it's because somewhere back in the process you have identified them incorrectly. In that case, you'll probably handle it similar to the way you handle the problem of having provided what the prospect feels is irrelevant or not helpful information.

Sample

Man, you are way off—we never have anything to do with that! Don't you know what we do here?

"I'm sorry that wasn't a good use of your time, I really hate it that I've used your time and not added any value to you. Would you be able to help me?"

I'll try.

"How could I have done better? What would you have included in there that wasn't there?"

Keep Them in Your Follow Up Group

Be careful not to push too hard at different points for the appointment. Or for information. The key to your success is that you provide high quality information to the prospect in the manner in which they are used to receiving it. He is not used to someone jumping out of his computer screen and telling him "Go here! Go there!" So, he is not going to respond positively when he perceives that you, as his information source, are trying to tell him what to do.

Too Much Work?

This might appear to be a lot of work. It is not. Not when you consider that you'll be selling more than you ever have. And by employing a few tools--laptop, e-mail, cell phone and web--much of the content you create can be leveraged and re-purposed for use in other modules and campaigns.

Part V: Objection-Handling

Chapter 15: **Questions and Listening**

Introduction

The prospect says "your price is too high" or "we're happy with what we've got" or just simply "I'm not interested." All common objections every salesperson has seen before. And while it's important to have a method for dealing with these objections when they come up, many salespeople feel it's even more important to have a solution for asking good, consultative questions in the first place.

JP Morgan famously once said "A man always has two reasons for doing anything: a good reason and the real reason."

Confusion

There is lots of confusion over objection handling in the sales world. Too much of the time, lip service is paid to the concept of asking good questions. And too much attention is given to the concept of objection handling, the act of quickly putting down customer objections as they arise. We are going to talk about Objection Handling and Good Questions; what it is, what it isn't and how to do it effectively in order to close the sales you want. Let me say something about Method here. The biggest take-away you should be getting out of this course is a consultative method to allow you to frame the types of questions you want to and to handle the toughest objections you get, all on your own and on demand.

Three Common Horrible Behaviors in Objection Handling

First, The OK-No problem! I will see what I can do!

This is where 90% of salespeople are today and that is a sad fact. Companies all over the country are putting salespeople into the field at high salaries and benefits, only to have them turn into go-fers who bring back lists of prospect's demands. What's the number one demand? Of course—lower your price! Lots of you watching this right now turn to this technique as your first and favorite and you need to stop that. We're giving you some approaches and you need to use them.

Next, The Defensive Eye-Darter

Looking pensive, he acts defensive, like he's trying to think of a way out of helping you, the prospect. What is actually going on of course is that the salesperson is struggling to think of a way to get the prospect to do what he wants. Only since the salesperson is not sure what it is he wants, or what it is the prospect WANTS to do, he's left looking like a shifty shmuck.

Finally, The Over-Complicating Sales Chump

Pushing out a façade of 'professionalism' to avoid looking like a chump, he ends up looking exactly like that. He relies on stalls and lengthy, babbling sentences which go nowhere, but which he hopes are really impressive. One salesperson I witnessed would answer each and every one of his own questions with another question! The prospect thinks "Man, does he think I am dumb?" Failure of Objection Handling has to do with the mindset around it. Objection Handling is contrary to the most successful thing salespeople do.

Successful salespeople are able to get the customer talking, sharing, and revealing what's important to them; Objection handling on the other hand is about stopping the customer, shutting them down, correcting them, shutting them up.

How are you going to build rapport, learn about your customer, become educated as to how he thinks, if you close him down, shut him up, prove to him his feelings, fears, thoughts, answers are all WRONG. Wrong because YOU have the answers, the right way of looking at things.

- Your price is too high--SHUT UP it is not.
- Your Quality isn't there…oh MAN you IDIOT yes it is!!
- Your service has been shoddy--WHAT? Are you even on the same planet?
- It doesn't work.

So much of training that focuses on Objection handling is about giving salespeople a false sense of control, holding out the holy grail that there is a BUTTON to push, a purple pill to take, that will keep the customer from telling you OTHER than what you want to hear. Because the old way was about winning some debate with the customer.

Now, why do we wonder when the customer shuts us off, stops talking to us, refuses to answer our calls, doesn't return emails when we have been cultivating this mindset all along?

The practice of getting people talking, of getting them comfortable to share with you is a lot more than them liking you. I assume most of you have been brought up in the sales profession to believe that if you get someone to like you will be all the more likely to sell to them. The rationale being that people buy from people they like. But its just as easy to say no to someone you like.

Nobody ever points that out, but it's true. So its not just about getting people to like you--and I assume you are already passably good at getting people to like if you have a sales job--

but about getting people in positions of authority to make decisions, to see the value of putting their business with you because you show them you can handle it and the way they know you can handle it is they had extensive conversations with you, learning about you, sharing with you what they needed and you sharing with them how you can provide that.

So how do you get someone to share with you? You have to engage them in conversation. You need to be able to have a conversation with them, one that by the way, you have a feeling you KNOW where its going, so you don't have to be surprised and confounded every time they answer a question or bring up a fact.

(How comfortable are you with someone when you share something with them and they are surprised or don't understand?)

So you need to know WHERE the conversation is going.

Well, how do you know, if you have never talked with this person before and if you are not at all sure how they do things?

Well, the answer is simple--you don't have to know the FACTS to be able to do this. In other words, knowing the FACTS, the names, the places, the length of time, the whys and etc. is NOT important, to you being able to carry on a CONVERSATION.

So, you need to study CONVERSATION rules and get comfortable knowing the flow and direction and rules of conversation; showing respect, empathy and credibility in CONVERSATION.

And that is what LANC™ is all about--helping you to visualize and gain foreknowledge of the conversation and its directions and rules before getting hung up on what the facts of the matter might be.

So we arrive at the fundamentals of Objection Handling;

1. Stay conversational.
    a. Don't kill rapport by being salesy
2. Be humble so as not to require BEING Humbled.
    a. Drop the façade—if you are confused admit it.
3. Seek to Understand BEFORE seeking to be understood.
    a. How many try to get the prospect to our side without knowing just what side the prospect is coming from.
    b. We need GOOD QUESTIONS and for good questions, you need to know WHERE you're leading the prospect.

The LANC™ Technique

What is LANC™

LANC™ is a method of questioning and listening. LANC™ is a simple, logical framework that follows the natural pattern of conversation avoiding gimmicky sales objection handling.

LANC™ is relationship-centric in that using it will strengthen your relationships with your prospects because LANC™ is a non-manipulative approach to communication.

LANC™ allows you to get what you want out of your sales calls because you can still be yourself using it.

Why Use LANC™

You should use LANC™ because a picture is worth a thousand words.

The Visual Verbal Conversion

Successful salespeople are those who are able to get their prospects to share information about problems and relevant facts surrounding the problem as it pertains to their solution. They are able to get the prospect to "draw them a picture" about the situation.

You may have found this is difficult to do and the reason why is something called the Visual-Verbal Conversion problem.

The Visual to Verbal Conversion Problem

When prospects have to describe a situation or problem or experience to a salesperson, they make a huge abbreviation in the facts. The reason why is that a picture is worth a thousand words and they don't want to spend the time or energy speaking a thousand words.

So 98% of those words that would describe the whole picture to you are held up. A kind of information dam is formed, where the prospect lets out a trickle of information, but holds back 98% of it for the sake of time and efficiency. Often, salespeople find that in the process of abbreviation, the prospect has left out information that the salesperson needs; how do you get this information? You develop rapport.

What Rapport is Not

Rapport is not poking around the prospects office and asking silly questions about the junk they store there. If you want to take your time hearing about the prospect's last fishing trip and hope doing that is going to get you the business, you're reading the wrong book.

Rapport is an experience of commonality between you and the prospect. It is evidenced by people who use the same types of words to describe similar experiences. You've got it when you and the prospect are on the same page; when you can ask questions which the prospect doesn't mind answering and might even enjoy doing so. You build rapport by getting the prospect involved in telling you something which is of importance to him, and give him the assurance that you are as interested in his description of it as he is.

Chapter 16: **The Optimal Situation: Psychological Fade**

The way to think about rapport for a salesperson is simple. Picture the prospect leaning back in his chair, looking at the ceiling and describing to the salesperson a situation. The salesperson listens. The prospect is now entirely focused on the situation in his own mind, the "picture" that only he can see; the salesperson and the current environment have faded into the background of the prospect's mind; a situation I call achieving "Psychological Fade."

The prospect now feels free to continue sharing. When the prospect pauses in his description, you as the salesperson might get him to continue with a brief one or two word question. Once you have the prospect describing a situation, the simpler your questions are, the more they can continue with the description. Simple questions tell the prospect "I can see what you can see." And simple means just that; Why? How? When? Who?

How to Lose Rapport

Vapid, sappy expressions and fake exclamations of "Wow!" or "Isn't that interesting!" will help you lose rapport. Complex questions disrupt rapport. When you ask an extended question of the prospect, you force him to break his concentration and focus on interpreting your question; he may do it, but he won't do much of it.

The Most Annoying People

Think of the last time you were in a social situation and had just met someone that you already couldn't stand being around. Maybe they were a nice person, a good person, a moral person; but they had this habit of wrenching everything you said over to a discussion from their point of view.

- "That reminds me of the time when I…"
- "Oh yes, well I think that…

That's why know-it-all salespeople fail; prospects simply cannot stand being around them. These types of salespeople think it's important to make prospects believe that they are always on top of what's being discussed—they think that asking any questions except those of the most sophisticated kind make them look stupid. Don't be one of them.

Body Language

Not all communication is verbal. As much as 80% of communication can be visual and there are some things you can do to use non-verbal communication to your advantage. Foot tapping, finger drumming and popping your pen are all examples of body language which can tell your prospect that you are nervous, uncomfortable or generally not to be trusted. Watch for them.

Chapter 17: **The Sphere of Concern**

The Sphere of Concern was developed to give salespeople a way to manage the process of first UNDERSTANDING an objection THEN handling it. The SoC works by giving you a way to visualize the concern underlying the objection; ultimately the issue that is at the Heart of the Matter.

The Sphere of Concern is that area of responsibility and or relevance to the prospect.

A CEO is concerned with issues such as survival, revenue growth, and profit. Because you cannot blurt out "Can we talk profit?" and expect to get anywhere consistently, you need to frame it. For a CEO you might focus your question on profits, company growth, survival, revenue, sales or investor perception, FOLLOWING THAT QUESTION to the heart of the matter. For the end- user of a piece of equipment you might focus on ease of use, reliability, how it makes his or her job easier.

Sphere of Concern: Levels

Going back to our JP Morgan quote, "A man always has two reasons for doing anything: a good reason and the real reason." The Sphere of Concern is a model of the prospect's issues and how those issues are communicated to the outside world and in particular to salespeople. Once you follow how the model works, you can use it to construct powerful strings of questions to allow your prospect to open up and tell you "the real reason."

Levels of the Sphere of Concern

1. Surface Concerns / Brush-off Objections: GOOMW (get out of my way)
2. Project or Initiative Level Concerns: I think this is the issue
3. Personal Credibility or Key Relationship Concerns: Here is what I've got to deal with / Who I deal with
4. Personal--Job Security / Compensation / Company Survival: I've GOT to;
    a. Grow sales
    b. Cut costs
    c. Improve Quality
    d. Improve safety

What You Hear

1. Surface Concerns / Brush-off Objections: GOOMW (get out of my way)
    a. They say things like: "I'm not interested; I have no time, we're happy with our current supplier; we have no need, no time, no problem, no budget."
2. Project or Initiative Level Concerns: I think this is the issue
    a. Most salespeople never routinely penetrate the first level, but when they do they can hear information which supports the first level Brush-Off statement; things like "We have a project

that's been prioritized and we cannot afford the time" or "Our supplier knows our business intimately, gives us the price points we need and is a highly trusted partner" or "There is no reason for us to consider any other options at this point, since we have no problems, no budget, no need."

3. Personal Credibility or Key Relationship Concerns: Here is what I've got to deal with / Who I deal with
    a. Only the very best salespeople get to this level with any consistency, but those who do will hear supporting concerns which are useful for re-directing the conversation; things like "Josh makes all of those decisions and I depend upon his support for my other initiatives and I need to keep him on my side, that's why I am not in a position to overrule him or come out against him on this."
4. Personal--Job Security / Compensation / Company Survival: I've GOT to;
    a. Finally, the heart of the matter concerns are reached by skillful handling of the conversation in each of the previous levels so that it becomes clear what the Personal Security or Heart of the Matter concerns are, how they are played into the objection or issue and how they support all the other concerns in the Sphere. Once these concerns are understood

Since there are so many layers to the prospect's issue or concern, can you see why typical objection handling approaches just fall flat and ineffective? To earn consultative seller's compensation you have to be able to BE consultative. And that means having some depth to your understanding and approach to solving the prospect's problems. Let's break down a typical surface objection by the levels of concern.

1. Your Price is too high (surface level concern)

2. Your competitor's price is cheaper by a large margin (if you get them to justify or give additional information as to their surface level concern it might be this.)
3. Your competitor quoted fewer options and I don't trust them as much and I am under pressure to cut costs and my I need my CFO's support for my OTHER major initiative and I don't understand how your solution is worth any more money and I don't have the time to figure it out. (If you can get them to share additional information under each of their previous levels of concerns it will involve additional related concerns of increasing complexity.)
4. I MUST keep costs low to KEEP my JOB! (if you can get them to a Heart of the Matter issue, you will find that personal security and well being concerns ranks at the top.)

You can see all the supporting concerns, which tie in to the initial brush off statement of "Your Price is too high." But you can also see that if you do NOT as a habit consistently get GOOD at breaking down and conducting good sales conversations around the prospects objection or surface concern, you might be tempted instead to just run BACK to your company and ask for a lower price to offer the customer. Note, also, that even if you GET the lower price from to offer them, that does NOT mean that you are now in a position to earn the business since SO MANY other concerns still are present which you did NOT address, first of all, because you didn't KNOW about them.

Another example we all hear is next.

1. Surface: We're happy with our current vendor
2. Project or Initiative-Level: They've been servicing us for 10 years I am sure you would feel the same
3. Personal Credibility / Key Relationship Concerns: Sure they've had issues and I would love to replace them with someone better, but what if you're worse and this means going against my subordinate and the IT team and I need their support for MY quality of life, and I don't understand how you could have that much of an impact.

4. Personal Job Security: I CANNOT afford service disruption costs!

Again, typical sales objection handling says to get involved in feature comparison and competitor bashing. Neither of which is the real issue here; of much greater value to you as a salesperson is to KNOW in this instance that Service Disruption Costs are HUGE concerns to this prospect; that these concerns are connected to his operation but also to very significant SOCIAL capital which is very important to him in his role.

Chapter 18: **Stages of LANC™**

The stages of the LANC™ process mirror the stages of the Sphere of Concern and allow you to play the part of the consultant in even the most demanding competitive pressure situations. Additionally, the structure of the LANC™ solution allows you to gain precious insight and foreknowledge of how a potential objection or question sessions will materialize so that you can fully anticipate and prepare for it.

Listen

The Listen step is about receiving the objection and showing that you are really listening to what the prospect is saying and thoughtfully considering a response.

Simple or Passive Listen's:

- OK
- I understand
- Right
- Mm-hmm
- Interesting

Reinforces that you are listening, that what they are saying is interesting to you that they should continue or keep on talking and sharing with you.

Supporting or Affirming Listen's:

- I see what you mean
- Thanks for sharing that
- I hear that alot

Builds rapport by showing obvious empathy for the prospect's articulation of the issue.

Abrupt or Game-Changer Listen's:

- It's not what you think!

This is used to STOP the prospect momentarily while you redirect the conversation.

Ask

The Ask is about having a good question to offer the prospect to move the conversation in the direction you want to go, to learn about the situation the prospect is facing and to close the deal.

Asking a good question is more about DIRECTION than it is about CONTENT. Content-based questions are more about getting the basic answers to Facts—how high, what color, how long, etc. On the other hand, simply knowing that you are here to solve problems means you only have to frame questions that lead to the discussion of problems or challenges in general.

For instance, a fundamental question could be "Of all your challenges in this area, which one concerns you the most right now?" You could anticipate further, and before even asking about challenges, an extremely simple, yet incredibly effective question I pull from interviewing candidates and that is "Where do you want to be in five years?" A variation of that is "Where do you want to be this time next year?"

Once the prospect begins answering that question, then your follow up question can be directed at those pesky issues which stand in his way of getting to where he wants to be in five years; "What do you see as the challenges or obstacles to getting you where you want to be in five years?"

Examples of Ask include;

- Where do you want to be in five years?
- If you could solve only one problem you face, what would it be?
- Who do you depend on most in accomplishing your objectives?

Combining Listen & Ask;

- I understand; do you mind if I ask you a question about that?
- OK; where in the process is that going to happen?

There are a great many ways to come up with good questions, many of which will be covered in detail throughout the course, particularly in the CLIENT™ qualification section. For now, depend use the Sphere of Concern to gain insight into your customer's problems and opportunities to come up with some good questions. Refer to the LANC™ Quick Reference chart on page 415 for assistance.

LANC™ Nudge

One of the most powerful ways to getting someone sharing additional information with you is skillful application of the Nudge technique. The Nudge technique is employed once you have the prospect's answer to one of your questions (Ask.) The Nudge is a simple, tiny version of an affirmation and a question. Examples of Nudge's;

- ✓ Really, why?
- ✓ Interesting, why that?

Remember what we talked about in terms of the Visual to Verbal conversion problem; that since a picture is worth a thousand words, if the prospect has to describe a situation to you, he is going to abbreviate it substantially rather than give you the thousand words.

Think of it this way—when you ask a really good question of the prospect, one that gets him thinking, imagine that there is a cartoon character bubble cloud over his head and him thinking about the question you gave him and how that question makes him think of so many other things so important to him.

While he is thinking this, you and his current surroundings psychologically fade (re achieving psychological fade) where you and his current surroundings fade in to the background while the powerful imagery invoked by the personal emotion he has for the situation that your great question made him think about—all of that comes to center stage in his mind.

Achieving psychological fade is a vital capability to the skilled salesperson because once you have achieved psychological fade, the prospect is yours to direct IF you use the right format, which the NUDGE is all about; simple, short, nurturing questions which simply prompt the prospect to continue his description of the picture he has in his mind.

Once you get the prospect sharing with you in this way, it is only with an EFFORT on HIS part, that he can STOP sharing. Doing this successfully will open up volumes of privileged information for you to access and to apply your own positioning of your solution to best help the prospect solve the problems he is facing.

Combining Listen & Ask & Nudge;

Listen: I understand.

Ask: When you say "Too expensive" how do you mean that?

[Prospect's responds]

Nudge: Really, why?

You will find your ability to get the prospect talking and sharing quality information with you to be almost so easy, it's almost unfair. That is the extreme consultative power contained in the tiny Nudge.

LANC™ Close

The close is not the hard close you may have been raised on, but a simple conclusion to the line of questions you have been asking. The LANC™ Close is how you gain assurance that you and the prospect are on the same page, going in the same direction.

Examples of LANC™ Close:

- So is it fair to say that _____?
- Does that make sense to you?
- Is that fair?
- Is that correct?

How to Move from No to Yes with Decision Points

Move a prospect from a certain "no" to a "yes" by using decision points. In this example you close for action, not for the sale.

Handling Objections with LANC™

Handling objections is about how to get a very busy prospect focused on your solution to his problem.

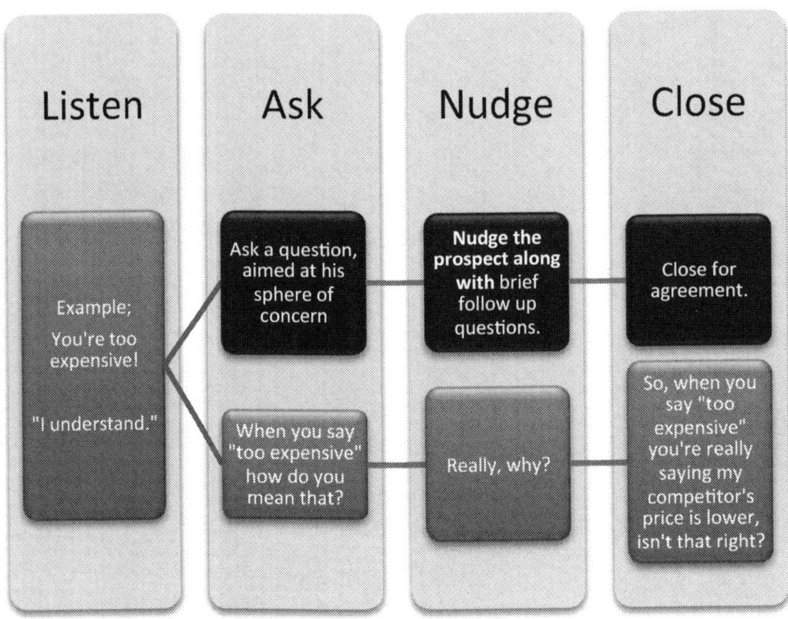

- ✓ **Listen**: show you are actively listening.
- ✓ **Ask**: Gets the discussion moving in a new direction with a statement or a question.
- ✓ **Nudge**: move in for more in-depth exploration or probing.
- ✓ **Close**: close for agreement to be sure you and the prospect are on the same page.

Objection: "You're too Expensive!"

- Listen:
  - "I understand."
- Ask
  - "Do you mind if I ask you a question?"
- Nudge
  - "When you say that you feel our pricing is not competitive, how do you mean that?"
  - *Your competitor is much cheaper.*
- Close
  - "Then, is it fair to say that you feel our pricing is high relative to the competitors offering, and not by itself based on the value we produce for you?"

"You're Still Too Expensive."

- Listen
  - "Hmmmmm..."
- Ask:
  - "I'm still 'too expensive?'"
- Nudge
  - "It sounds like you don't agree with how we've priced our solutions, doesn't it?"
  - *I can't answer for how you decided to set your prices, I'm just saying that I can't see spending that much.*
  - "Really? Why?"
  - *I just can't see how it's worth it.*
- Close
  - "It sounds like what you're saying is you don't think the ROI is there; is that fair?"
  - *That's exactly what I'm saying.*
  - "Then we need to talk about the ROI, because all that information is based on what you gave me."

Conclusions

Often, the real trick in effective questions and objection handling is simply about getting the prospect to move from an impossible objection to being able to correct the objection with information which the prospect wasn't considering.

Part VI: Sales Qualification

Chapter 19: **About Sales Qualification**

What is Sales Qualification?

Sales Qualification is the discipline of measuring the probability of the prospect to buy. It involves applying a set of characteristics to the prospect and profiling them along a standard profile.

If the comparison comes up short, the prospect is said to be unqualified—if you actively discourage the prospect from further consideration or cut them off entirely you are qualifying out the prospect (who actually then would be said to not be a prospect at all for your solution.)

If the prospect meets the requirements then you continue to invest the necessary time to sell to them, since you have "qualified" the prospect as being a good use of your time and resources.

Highly Valued

Good sales qualifying is something that every sales organization wants to do better. Getting to the point where ultimately you are able to rapidly determine if you should be selling to a particular prospect means you are able to free yourself from investing time—wasting time—selling to "unqualified" prospects (suspects) and spend more or even all of your time selling to those prospects most likely to buy from you.

Problems with Qualifying

Fear

Salespeople are often afraid to ask qualifying questions as they reason the prospect will not want to continue with the sales process with them if they show they are too interested in making the sale.

Too harsh

Qualifying questions can justify the salesperson's fear above when they are delivered too harshly, as is often the case with salespeople who are uncomfortable in asking the question in the first place. Think of the admonition to not be afraid to "ask the tough questions" and you can see the point. (And what is the number one reason salespeople are reluctant to bring their sales managers into their opportunities?)

Too soft

Qualifying that is too soft is also problematic; first in that it does not actually qualify the prospect but more so because the salesperson will think the prospect *is* qualified and will conduct a time consuming and expensive sales process on the basis of such soft qualification.

Sales Bias

When the salesperson asks a qualifying question of the prospect it is most often from the perspective or interest of the salesperson. Prospects do not like and do not put up with much of this type of qualifying, as it is intimidating.

Misguided

Salespeople are often asking qualifying questions which do not actually qualify the prospect.

> "How do we stand?"
> "How do we look?"
> "Are we in the range?"

Too many questions are vacuous, empty questions that the prospect can often deflect with similarly vacuous responses—"All things being equal you look fine."

Qualification versus Persuasion

Qualifying is what you do when you assess or test a prospect; persuading is what you do when you attempt to win the prospect to your viewpoint. What happens in most selling situation is these two are separate; the salesperson persuades for a while, and then asks a qualifying question, holds his breath, gets the answer, exhales and goes back to persuading.

The Best Qualification

The best qualification takes place without the prospect knowing or feeling that they are being qualified and which puts the salesperson in a position of power with the prospect by earning his respect of you as an expert. Qualifying in this manner is only possible by focusing on the underlying business ramifications and conditions that the prospect is always concerned with but may not believe or be aware of your solutions impact on.

These business conditions are affected not only by your solution, but also by the manner in which the prospect conducts a sales process to consider the purchase of your solution and ultimately rationalizes his decision to purchase that solution.

Knowing these conditions and structuring the positioning of your solution will enable you to behave almost as a mind reader as you sell "perfectly" to the qualified prospect and discontinue selling to unqualified prospects.

Chapter 20: **Introducing the CLIENT™ Qualification Index**

Sales happen when prospects are willing and able to change costly problems by allocating money to the best solution in a timely manner.

The CLIENT™ Qualification index is the grouping of the six elements present in any decision of any prospect to purchase anything and structuring the positioning of your solution to incorporate them.

Buyer's Equity

You've heard of Buyer's Remorse? Buyer's Remorse is the sinking feeling after the sale that the purchase might not meet the needs for which it was purchased, leading the Buyer to regret, or to feel remorse, for having bought the solution.

There's something that happens prior to the sale that drives the buyer towards buying in the first place; something I call Buyer's Equity.

Before a prospect can buy from you, he must first be made ready to buy. In order to make the major decision to buy, the prospect first makes a series of lesser decisions. "Will this product solve my problem? Is it better than the alternative? When will I see a return on my investment?" The answers determine his readiness to buy your solution, or his Buyer's Equity for your solution.

Like the equity in your home, Buyer's Equity works under a similar principle. As the salesperson makes "payments" of information to the prospect, the goodwill of the prospect for the salespersons solution goes up; the Equity that the Buyer has for the solution increases.

When Buyer's Equity is too low, there will not be a sale made to this prospect.

If you can consistently build high levels of Buyer's Equity for your solution, your prospects will buy your solutions and at a higher margin than your competitor who does not build Buyer's Equity.

The Six Parts of Buyer's Equity

Sales happen when prospects are willing and able to change costly problems by allocating money to the best solution in a timely manner. Sales occur when the following six attributes are present, as indicated above.

1. Stated Willingness
2. Ability, in terms of Decision Makers involvement
3. Problems are Quantified as to Cost
4. Return on Investment is Quantified
5. Specification Rules for the Best Solution is Identified
6. Timeline for the Sales Process is Outlined

The CLIENT™ Qualification Index

There are six parts to Buyer's Equity; therefore, there are six elements to the CLIENT™ Qualification Index.

Sales happen when prospects are willing (Commitment) and able (Leadership) to change costly problems (Impact) by allocating money (Economics) to the best solution (Need) in a timely manner (TimeLine).

Commitment

Commitment is the readiness of your prospect to assure you of their willingness to do something in accordance with your sales process. When you ask the prospect to meet with you and he agrees, that is one type of commitment. When the prospect agrees to purchase your solution if it is able to perform well in some form of testing is another (awesome) commitment. Ultimately, the prospect's willingness to change the current way they are doing something and use your solution to do something in a new way is what you need to assess constantly. Getting consistent commitment from the prospect during your sales process is essential to any qualifying.

Leadership

The team of people involved in making the decision to purchase your solution is essential qualifying information. At what level will the final decision be made—the CEO? What level are you dealing and hoping to sell to? Someone so far down in the organization that has barely met the CEO? How well qualified is your prospect if that is the case? Many more items are considered here and will be dealt with in more detail.

Impact

What is the cost of the problem that your solution removes? Many salespeople need to re-read that line before it begins to sink in. Having a problem is not enough—the prospect must have a cost associated with *not* having your solution that is considerably larger than the price associated with acquiring it for them to even consider talking with you. Being able to ascertain that your solution will remove enough cost—in hard dollars, soft dollars, in efficiency, productivity, safety, morale and however else they measure it—is essential to being able to demonstrate the value of your solution.

Economics

Anything that has to do with the monies around purchasing your solution is in the Economics category. Items such as sufficient budgets, paper path of approval, requisition process, terms, discounts, ROI (return on investment), any and all financial numbers used to qualify your solution are covered here.

Need

Need is one of the most effective and powerful of all qualifiers and odds are it does not mean what you have grown up thinking it means. A need is most often defined as a problem as used in this sentence "They are in big trouble the way they do it now, so there is quite a need for our solution." Typically, salespeople tend to confuse their definition of a problem with their understanding of a need.

A customer can have a problem and still not have a *need* for your solution. Otherwise there would never be a situation where a customer buys the wrong solution to their perceived problem.

A need is defined as that which provides the best solution to their problem, *as they understand it*, not as you think it. Therefore, qualifying the prospect for your solution will involve an intimate understanding of their Specification Rules—those items they feel should be found in the pre-sales presentation of your solution and the way in which they will ultimately judge whether those items are present.

TimeLine

The TimeLine is that all-important schedule of events that culminate in the decision. Too many times, salespeople lose opportunities because they miscalculate how much time they have to land the deal. Understanding the TimeLine is essential to successful qualifying.

Problems and Challenges with CLIENT™

Sometimes salespeople are afraid of using CLIENT™ because they fear that CLIENT™ does not take into account all the things necessary to sell to the prospect. This is a demonstrably false assumption.

- ✓ When is it not relevant to secure commitment? When is it smart to not care about the willingness of the people to make a change? (Commitment)
- ✓ When does it make sense in the sales process to not pay attention to who the decision makers are, what the organizational chart looks like, who is making a final decision, who is influencing a decision and who is dead set against that decision? (Leadership)
- ✓ When does it make sense to try to sell something without understanding the prospects problems, the cost of those problems and the causes of those problems? (Impact)
- ✓ When does it make sense to not pay attention to the prospect's ability to pay, their desired ROI, so you know whether your solution's price is going to float? (Economics)

- ✓ When does it make sense to not pay attention to the way the customer will make his decision, the various requirements he is going to look at to make that decision and your perceived value versus your competitors? (Need)
- ✓ When does it make sense to not pay attention to the timing of the deal? When does it make sense to not pay attention to compelling events on the prospects schedule which—surprise!--may take priority over your own solution? (TimeLine)

CLIENT™ is all you need, because that's all the customer is going to consider. What you want to do is to arrange the information requirements that are particular to your industry or your company within it. The CLIENT™ model is flexible; most of the differentiating things that you're going to consider--such as your product specifications or the variations particular to your own unique solution--are going to be readily accommodated within its framework.

Chapter 21: **Commitment**

What is Commitment?

Commitment is when you ask for confirmation from your prospect on something.

Why Get Commitment?

Commitment is about making sure that you and prospect are on the same page and going in the same direction. It is not about hard closing, aggressive, pushy, in your face selling.

It simply refers to the consistent practice of making sure, through confirmation that you are aware of the direction the prospect wishes to go in.

It means that you institute a consistent practice of making sure that you both understand each other.

It is important that you secure commitment to ensure that your time and resources are being spent in the best possible way. It is also important because you do not want to be surprised by the prospect telling you that he never had any intention of buying after you have done a tremendous amount of work, and that the reason why you didn't know that was because you never asked for a commitment.

If you consistently proceed to sell without securing commitment, you'll find that your ability to spend more time with quality prospects and less time with non-purchasing prospects will be totally compromised. Not because you don't have a superior solution, not because you're not a good person, not because you don't represent a good company; but because you never ask the prospect to make a decision.

Commitment: When?

When you should get commitment is prior to spending a lot of your time, money or resources. For instance if the prospect asks you to fly to Timbuktu for a presentation, you would probably want to confirm a few of the details and certainly what the next steps might be as result of your having complied with his request.

If the prospect asks you to submit a proposal, you might want to understand what happens after you do that.

If the prospect asks you to loan him your solution in the form of an evaluation for a period of time, you probably want to know for what purpose and what will happen afterwards (for instance, will a purchase result or is this for charitable purposes?)

Key Commitment Questions

- ✓ "I am planning on 60 minutes for this meeting; does that still work for you?"
- ✓ "Once we're done, you should know enough about us to either decide to take the next step, or maybe that now is not the right time. OK?"

- ✓ "What I was hoping to accomplish today is this [your objective]; does that sound fair?"
- ✓ "When I do [that], will you be in a position to do [this]?"
- ✓ "Once [that]'s done, do you think the next step might be [this]?"
- ✓ "What is the best way to accomplish that?"
- ✓ "Why don't we get started now?"

Examples of Commitment

Securing the Pre-Call

Prior to meeting with the prospect for the first time, you should try to set up a phone call to review what you are planning to talk about and to be sure you are prepared.

- ✓ "Would you help me make the most of this upcoming time with you?"

OK.

- ✓ "Would you take a call from me next week to briefly review the meeting agenda and allow me to incorporate any changes before I show up? Takes about 7-11 minutes."

Can you email me your questions?

- ✓ "I can, but a brief discussion might be simpler, just to be better prepared. Is that OK?"

Sure.

Starting the Meeting

A quick and effective way to start meetings with prospects is below.

- ✓ "Thanks for taking the time to meet with me. What I planned for was about 45 minutes. Does that still work for you?"
- ✓ "What I was hoping we could accomplish was to share some information about what I do, to learn a bit about what's important to you and decide together where to go from there."
- ✓ "Does that sound acceptable to you? Is there anything you'd prefer to focus on first?"

Pre-Proof

Before you invest substantial time and energy into writing a proposal you should get commitment that you and the prospect are seeing mutual value in the exercise.

- ✓ "If I were to put the resources into providing a full proposal for you, would you be able to just be sure of one thing?"

Sure. What?

- ✓ "That if you wanted to buy it, there is nothing to prohibit you from buying it within the time period?"

Aggressive Next Step Scheduling

In hyper-competitive industries where the chances are high that your prospect will not meet with you again, try to schedule the next meeting before you begin the first. Use a relaxed, almost humorous disposition when applying this, as it is a heavy technique.

- ✓ "When am I coming back?"

What do you mean?

- ✓ "I mean, once you've seen how much we can help you, if you're like most people, you may want a more complete understanding in another meeting. So why don't we schedule that now?"

Well, I might decide I don't want to meet with you again…

- ✓ "If you decide you don't want to, we'll cancel it. But, let's go ahead and schedule that now. OK?"

Preventing Short-Changing

Ever have a prospect tell you at the beginning of the appointment that something has come up and now they only have 15 minutes? You know that your value cannot be conveyed in such a short time and that worse, the prospect will feel that because value was not conveyed, that it was because you don't have any and not that he didn't give you enough time.

In that case, the only thing to do is not give the prospect the opportunity to decide that you have no value, but to reschedule the appointment. Here's how.

I've only got 15 minutes.

- ✓ "Do you mind if I ask you a question?"

Sure.

- ✓ "When you say 'you've only got 15 minutes,' how do you mean that?"

I can't spend the hour with you today—I have a budget meeting come up.

- ✓ "So you were hoping I could give my presentation to you in 15 minutes?"

Yes.

- ✓ "Not possible and it wouldn't be fair to you to try. Why don't we reschedule?"

Key Commitment Tool: The Agenda.

What is an Agenda

An agenda is a list of meeting topics, a meeting roadmap. It covers information you are going to present and is a sort of rulebook for the conduct of the meeting. It may include options for proceeding and suggested next steps.

Why Use an Agenda

Using an agenda will help you avoid the pitfalls of run-on-forever meetings or occasions when the prospect seizes control from you. It ensures the topic you want to cover will be covered in detail. It also conveys professionalism and respect for the prospect and his time.

As simple as the agenda is, it takes some salespeople a long time to figure out to begin to use one and then to use one effectively. Even the most basic agenda suggests to the prospect that you are serious about your time and about their time. Get in the habit of preparing an agenda for every meeting and sharing that with the prospect before you start.

For significant meetings--such as proposal or contract finalization—you will want to qualify the agenda by phone prior to showing up and conducting the meeting. That way any changes the prospect wants you to incorporate can be done with adequate time for you to implement the change.

Create an Agenda

Create an agenda for an upcoming meeting. Consider;

- ✓ What is the purpose of the meeting?
- ✓ What will you do?
- ✓ What do they need to do?
- ✓ What are the Take-Aways?
- ✓ What are the next steps?
- ✓ How do you determine if they should be taken?

Your Meeting Plan will guide you through this process.

Sample Agenda

A sample agenda might look like the one below.

- Introductions
- Company Background
- Project Review
- Corporate Overview
- Presentation
- Questions and Answers
- Next Steps Commitment
- Conclusion
- Exit

Working the Agenda

Use the agenda to layout your plans for the meeting with the prospect and close for their agreement.

- ✓ "Here's what we're here to do…(1,2,3…)"
- ✓ "Would you agree that's a good objective?"

Sure.

- ✓ "Would you add anything?"

No.

- ✓ "Remove anything?"

No, looks fine.

Closing on the Agenda.

- ✓ "So, completing this, what happens next?"

Well, I'm not sure.

- ✓ "May I make a suggestion?"

OK.

- ✓ "The next step should be [insert next step.]"

Remember

Commitment is when you ask for confirmation from your prospect on something; nothing more.

Chapter 22: **Leadership**

What is CLIENT™ Leadership?

The Leadership category is all about the people in your prospect's company who are involved in the decision to purchase your solution.

Understanding who they are, what their relationships are with one another, what their power is within the organization and what their level of accessibility is are all vital concerns for the professional salesperson. Knowing how to provide the information they need to see your solution's benefits in the light of how those benefits will help them to get what they want is crucial to your success.

Titles versus Roles

You may have already seen that there is a significant difference between the titles of decision makers in one company from the titles of those same decision makers for your solution in another company.

Effectively managing the decision for your solution involves being able to separate titles that are given by companies from roles that are relevant to your sales cycle.

Titles

Titles are assigned by the organization based on the job description and responsibility that the organization has placed in that position and under that title. The title has relevance to the company and to the state of its organization chart. It may not have any relevance to what you sell, particularly as you sell to different organizations. For example, the decision maker for your solution in one company may be the Chief Operating Office; in another company you sell to the decision maker may be the VP of Finance.

Examples of titles include;

- VP Procurement
- Director of Purchasing
- Vice President Purchasing
- VP Finance
- CFO
- COO

While you may find that the titles of your decision makers vary greatly from one company to the next, you may also find that you enjoy selling to one type of title more than to another and that you tend to be more successful with one type of title than another.

Roles

Roles are different from titles, as roles are assigned by the salesperson based on the relevance of the role to the sales cycle. Like titles, roles have certain responsibilities that are associated with them, as far as the sales cycle is concerned.

Unlike titles, roles do not change from sales cycle to sales cycle nor do they change from company to company. The role of ultimate decision maker--Mr. Big--does not change from one sales cycle to the next. There is always a Mr. Big.

Similarly, there is almost always a Campaigner, that individual who sees a personal victory in having your solution purchased by his company. In those sales cycles where you have no Campaigner, you will probably have no sale.

Multiple roles can sometimes be filled by the same individual; for example, sometimes Mr. Big and the Campaigner is the same person--an enviable position for you as their salesperson to be in.

Functions and Definitions of Key Roles

Final Approval

The person in charge of the company is usually the final word in any acquisition decision. Finding out who this person is and ensuring your business case is in line with their business objectives is one of the keys to your sales success.

Allies

We need them in war, in peace and definitely in sales. Who is going to help you make your business case to the company and on behalf of the company? Who is the internal salesman for your solution when you're not around?

Opposition

Every major purchase decision made by a company has an opponent; otherwise the solution wouldn't need a salesperson like you. Find out who they are and what plans your allies have to either befriend them or to defeat them and how you can help.

Roles Defined

Mr. Big

Mr. Big is your final authority on the decision. Many times he is the CEO or president. He is important because he is the agenda-setter for the entire organization. If you want someone to pay attention to a particular project, he can direct that individual to do so. He has enormous influence if not direct control over which projects get funding. He can make the case to reallocate funding to non-budgeted initiatives if necessary. He ultimately owns the decision and will ensure due diligence prior to allowing his organization to purchase anything of significance.

He is immensely important to both the initiation of and the conclusion of your sales process.

Campaigner

More than just someone who is in favor of you and for your solution, your Campaigner has a personal interest in your solution being bought; he also has some authority in the company.

Make sure you have not incorrectly identified him. Don't designate someone simply because he is the first one you spoke to. Many times your enemy in the account is the first person you might be meeting with.

The Campaigner for your solution is someone who has a vested interest in seeing your solution be put in place and also holds some authority to make it happen. Your Campaigner ultimately will go to the line for your solution and fight for it if it comes down to it.

Moneyman

Typically the CFO is going to be your Moneyman. The Moneyman is most concerned with the economics of the solution, the financial numbers that explain your solution in terms of its pure value to the cash flow of the business. He is dead set against any type of feature description or technical justification. He wants to see bottom line and only bottom line results.

Enemy

The Enemy wants to see your solution NOT be picked.

He is the antithesis of your Campaigner in that he has a personal win in seeing your sale fail and has some authority or credibility to make that happen if he gets the chance.

Your Enemy sees costs to your solution that others do not. For some, your solution may mean more work or accountability. For others your solution may threaten his job security based on automation or some other efficiency that your solution brings. They may be in favor of the status quo or they may want to see another solution they are championing is purchased.

Finally, they may simply be political enemies of your Campaigner and are opposed to whomever he recommends.

Victim

The victim is the individual or individuals who are most dramatically affected by the problems that your solution is going to remove. That means they're also the biggest benefactors of your solution being picked. It is extremely helpful to find out who these people are and to get their input. Many times they are either closely related to or are the Campaigner himself.

Riddler

If your solution is a technical solution, or a software application or service for the information technology department, you often have to deal with a technical expert inside the account. You can call him the Riddler, because he is simply loaded with questions. Many of which seem designed to trip you up; sometimes they actually are. Don't verbally spar with the Riddler; no sales double talk—just keep pure, undecorated information flowing in his direction.

Key Leadership Questions

There are several questions that can be used to get information in the Leadership category addressed.

- ✓ "How did you get started in this business?"
- ✓ "Where do you want to be this time next year? In five years?"
- ✓ "What is the key to getting there?"
- ✓ "If you don't, what do you think will have prevented you?"
- ✓ "What's the key to someone being successful in a position like yours?"
- ✓ "What's the key to being viewed as successful in your position?"
- ✓ "Competition for funding can be fierce; who do you look to for help in justifying your decisions?"
- ✓ "Who do you expect to challenge your funding requests?"
- ✓ "Every company has a team of people to inspect purchase decisions; in some cases, each one of these people has to sign off on any requisition—who are they here?"
- ✓ "When you want to get something done, who inspects your decision?"

- ✓ "How involved do they like to be early in the process?"
- ✓ "How involved does management like to get in your decisions?"
- ✓ "What's the key to working with them?"
- ✓ "How do you describe your role here?"

Key Tool: the Organizational Chart

An organizational chart can be very helpful in getting an understanding of the account. An organizational chart can serve as an excellent source of strategy; among other things you can use it for placing your contact within the chart and anticipate some of the challenges he will run into in getting your solution purchased.

How to Get an Org Chart

There are several ways to acquire an organizational chart. You can build one, using available online resources.

Or you can ask your prospect for one; often they will be only too happy to give one to you, so long as you they trust your use of it. Ask;

- ✓ "Can I have one?"

You can involve your prospect in putting one together, by assembling one to the best of your ability and presenting it to the prospect asking;

- ✓ "I made one; how am I doing?" and let the prospect tell you what needs fixing.

Finally, you can begin to draw one while they speak, asking questions as you do so. If you do this, simply ask for the titles that are involved with the decision first. Later you can come back and request the first names and put them next to the appropriate titles.

- ✓ "Do you mind if make I note of their first names?"

The last step would be to come back around and add last names as they come up in your discussion. This will prevent you from triggering discomfort or fear in the prospect that can happen when you try to get all the information upfront and at once.

Also, as you are going through the org chart and asking questions you can add more information to each contact as the prospect is discussing that contact. Ask questions like;

- ✓ "How long has he been here?"
- ✓ "How would you typify your working relationship?"
- ✓ "How much do they contribute to your success?"

Calling on Mr. Big

Getting Mr. Big involved early in your sales cycle can be a highly effective way to reduce your sales cycle length and increase your close ratios.

There are several reasons to call on Mr. Big, many of which were covered in the prospecting section on calling high. You will revisit them here briefly.

Agenda Setter

Mr. Big is the agenda setter for his organization. If he has something he needs his executive team or other subordinates to pay attention to he can ask and they will.

If Mr. Big is impressed enough by your call to either refer you to someone in his organization, or even meet with you himself, you can bet you have a leg up on the competition. If he refers you to someone that works for him, you can be sure they will pay more attention to your voicemail stating you just spoke with their CEO than to your competitor's voicemail.

Get Information Subordinates Do Not Have

Also, you can get information that subordinates do not have as it pertains to your solution. Contacting Mr. Big directly and asking him a few questions means you can then direct his answers to whomever is in charge of viewing your solution and making a decision on it.

Consider the following scenario when, even with Mr. Big's reference, a stubborn subordinate is attempting to put you off;

We don't really have any need for that now; we have the XYZ project to attend to first.

"Really? Mr. Big suggested that based on the fact that the XYZ project was close to wrapping up, that he thinks it would be a good use of time for us to meet sooner. Do you disagree?"

No, I don't disagree. If he thinks we should give it some attention sooner, then we will. When do you want to come by?

Gain Peer Basis with Officers

You can gain a peer basis with other company officers that you may have to deal with now or later on in your sales process. In the case of VPs and other company officers, only their peers speak with Mr. Big about business matters. So you are in their peer group for now. When you contact Mr. Big you become "the guy that Mr. Big brought in" to employees.

Competition is Limited

Very few salespeople try to contact Mr. Big, so you will enjoy limited competition. Your sales cycle will run smoother and faster with fewer ultimate objections. You will have momentum!

Selling to Mr. Big

Start Early

You want to sell to Mr. Big early and often enough to keep him updated on your progress, but not too much that you become a liability for him. Consensus in his organization is important to Mr. Big and you do not want to give the impression that you are using him to steamroll a solution into the company.

Keep Him Updated

Keep the information flowing to him in small pieces with moderate frequency. Do not try to do the job of his subordinates in evaluating and making the decision regarding your solution. By keeping him as a resource and not overusing the access to him, he can be your ace in the hole when you run into an uncooperative decision team that may be giving your competitor an unfair advantage.

What to Sell to Him

Mr. Big is responsible for the bigger picture; the grand vision for the company usually comes from him. So keep your solution advantages described in terms of Business Improvement. Growth and profitability are sure bets, as are competitiveness and business survival depending on the industry. Cost reduction can play in, but be sure it is significant enough; unlike the Moneyman, Mr. Big is often quite alright with cost in the short run, so long as his big vision is in focus.

His Key Business Objective

Knowing Mr. Big's Key Business Objective is the key to knowing Mr. Big. You don't need to know that he likes to golf, or to sail, or to fly if you know the KBO that he watches to keep his business on track (and which allows him to golf, sail, fly, etc.)

As far as learning what that KBO is, you cannot simply blurt out a request for him to tell you what it is; sometimes salespeople are surprised to learn that he doesn't *know* what it is. You can ask questions like;

- ✓ "What do you want to see happen in your business over the next five years? And what over the next 12 months?"
- ✓ "Where do you want to be in five years?"
- ✓ "If you make it, what will be the One Key Thing to getting there?"
- ✓ "What is the most important thing to that One Key Thing happening?"

It's an easy way to drill down into what makes Mr. Big tick. Sure, you run the risk of him getting gruff with you and asking;

What kind of question is that?

But the risk is worth the gains you receive.

Mr. Big's Go-To Team

More questions for Mr. Big. These will help you understand whom he turns to in the organization to make things happen. You can learn a lot about whom he likes, whom he trusts and who can help you with these questions.

- ✓ "When you want to get something done, whom do you turn to?"
- ✓ "There's tons of competitive pressure today—how do you prepare your people to compete?"

- ✓ "How do you find people with that kind of competitive drive in them?"
- ✓ "How do you ensure people are doing the job you want them to?"

Spot-Check ROI

One way to determine if the solution you are selling has sufficient visibility and sponsorship at Mr. Big's level is to ask a question that shows his readiness to allocate budget; but of course not in a way that is too obvious. In this case, assume he is referring you to someone in his organization—let's call him Sam—to evaluate your solution.

- ✓ "If Sam were to bring a $50,000 requisition for my solution to you, what kind of ROI would need to be there for you to approve it?"

For a solution like yours I'd want to see a 200% return in the first year.

- ✓ "Really? Why?"

It's not currently a priority and it would have to be that good to get our attention.

- ✓ "It sounds like what you're saying is that you'll approve Sam if he can point to a 200% ROI; is that fair?"

You can customize this for other areas of business impact that your solution may provide, such as;

- o Risk aversion
- o Loss
- o Business Continuance

Selling and Your Campaigner

Your Campaigner is another key to your sale. In the above example we saw a lot about making Mr. Big effectively be your Campaigner. Sometimes that is realistic, but most often it is someone else in the organization who will be responsible for evaluating your solution.

Campaigner Review

Some facts about what and who a Campaigner is;

- ✓ Wants to see you win the account
- ✓ Has a personal, vested interest in your solution
- ✓ Has some Authority in the company
- ✓ Do not be too hasty to identify him—this is a common error with overanxious salespeople
- ✓ Will go to the line for your solution and fight for you

Finding a Campaigner

Finding your Campaigner can be difficult.

The best way to locate him is a downstream referral from Mr. Big. The second best way is in the form of a peer referral, where you start with a VP or Director possibly even in another department.

The least effective way to find your Campaigner is to start with one of his subordinates and attempt to get referred upstream to him. Again, while this is the most common way of getting in touch with someone who could be your Campaigner, it is the also the least effective.

Qualifying Your Campaigner

Be sure you actually have a Campaigner and not someone masquerading as a Campaigner. Pay attention to questions in the following areas;

- Campaigner's Visions for the business?
- Campaigner's where in 5 years?
- Campaigner's View of the problem?
- Campaigner's View of the solution?
- What does he like about what we do?
- Campaigner's Power Grid (his Go-to Relationships)
- Campaigner's Relationship with Mr. Big
- Campaigner's Personal Plan to Befriend/Defeat Opponent

Questions for Your Campaigner

Similar to Mr. Big, thought you can go into a lot more detail in the depth and length of your questions; your Campaigner has more time to think and talk about your solution since it is a lot closer to his job description than to Mr. Big's.

- ✓ "How did you get this job?"
- ✓ "Where do you want to be in five years? This time next year?"
- ✓ "How does this problem affect your ability to get there?"
- ✓ "How do you describe your role here?"
- ✓ "What do you tell your friends you do for work?"
- ✓ "What's the key to someone being successful in a position like yours?"
- ✓ "What's the key to being viewed as successful in your position?"

Campaigner's Kryptonite

Communicate clearly and accurately with your Campaigner regarding your solution and any and all commitments you make to him. There is nothing like taking the fight out of your Campaigner than the following errors salespeople commonly commit;

- Wrong Facts
- Ignorance of Key Business Objectives

- Information unrelated to Key Business Objectives
- Enemy better informed
- Missed deadlines

All of these items weaken his ability to make a high-credibility business case.

Remember

The Leadership category is all about the people in your prospect's company who are involved in the decision to purchase your solution. Your job as a professional salesperson is to identify who they are and sell to them on the basis of their own stake in the solution.

Chapter 23: **Impact**

What is Impact?

Impact is the cost of the problem that your solution removes.

Why is Impact Important?

Impact is used as the baseline for your solution's value.

About Impact

Impact is the COST of the problem, not just the problem itself. This is a critical distinction. Too many salespeople view the fact that the customer has a problem that "must be costing them something" as a sufficient foundation for the customer to base a purchase decision upon.

It is not.

Most solutions today that require salespeople to sell them are high priced solutions, mission critical solutions. These solutions are not bought without careful examination, consensus and validation on the part of the prospect and his company.

The days of selling features and benefits are long past—now the prospect must be able to describe your solution's value in bottom line, non-technical benefits to the company. Non-technical business decision makers are always involved in the consensus to allocate money to solutions that can provide significant business value, and they are not interested in hearing about technical descriptions. As a matter of fact, it makes them nervous.

So Impact is the means by which you begin to convey your solution's value to the prospect in terms of bottom line business benefits.

Why the name?

It measures the Impact of your solution in terms of the bottom line business benefits to the prospect; the cost of the problem which your solution removes. If your solution reduces downtime on a production line, you would assess the value which your solution provides in terms of the dollars saved by having less downtime. So if downtime costs the organization $10,000 per hour and you can prove that your solution will reduce downtime by 10 hours per month, your solutions Impact is $100,000 per month (10 hrs. x $10,000 per hour) or $1.2 million per year ($100,000 x 12 months.)

Using Impact enables salespeople to align their solution's price alongside value gained from that solution. You can now compete against the volume of return on investment—ROI—instead of your competitor's cheap price.

Without Impact

Without Impact, there is NO basis for establishing your value in the account. If you cannot convey bottom line business value that your solution delivers to your prospect's business it won't get bought consistently. If you cannot convey bottom line value efficiently, it doesn't get bought fast enough for you to be able to carry on enough simultaneous sales cycles to make your numbers. And those cycles you do carry on will take a long time to close, while you slug it out over price with other cheaper competitors.

Examples of Impact Areas

There are a great many different ways to assess Impact. These can include;

- ✓ Speed
  - Time to Market
  - Productivity
  - Efficiency
- ✓ Costs
  - Scrap
  - Rework
  - Risk
  - Safety
- ✓ Quality
  - Improvements
  - Gains in New Sales
  - New Customers

Find the NIGHTMARE Scenario

Car insurance, seat belts, annual physicals, life insurance and smoke alarms. All are examples of little sometimes annoying things we purchase or perform to avoid the nightmare situation that could happen as a result of not doing them. What is the potential nightmare scenario your solution removes?

Key Impact Questions

Early in Your Sales Process

- ✓ How do you do that now?
  - Why do you do it that way?
  - How long have you done it that way?

- ✓ Is there a better way?
    - o What are the problems with doing it that way?
    - o How does doing it that way affect your ability to do your job?
- ✓ How does that problem make itself known?
- ✓ What's keeping you up at night?
    - o Can you live with that?

Deeper Impact Questions

As you become more involved in the sales process, you can begin to ask deeper Impact questions. Questions like the ones below are typically reserved for steps in the MAJOR™ Sales Process, particularly the MAJOR™ Audit, which is covered in later chapters.

- ✓ Step me through that process?
    - o What happens then?
    - o How long does that take?
    - o How much does that cost?
    - o How do you measure cost here?
- ✓ Is that a big problem?
    - o Is that a big enough problem to spend money on fixing?
    - o How much money/time would that save you if it were not a problem anymore?
    - o How easy is that to do?
- ✓ What if the solution fails?
    - o What happens if you can't start on time?

In Your World

Your CLIENT Map™ is not a static document, but one that you should consistently work, adding new questions, customizing your CLIENT™ categories.

Think about Impact in your world and come up with some specific examples of what Impact looks like.

What are your Key Impact items? Are they the same for most prospects? How do you ask for them? How do you handle objections? Record them in your CLIENT Map™.

The Cost of the Whole Problem

Impact is the cost of the whole problem. Consider the problems that your solution solves; what are these problems and what are some examples of them?

What are some related problems? Every problem, such as downtime in a production line, has related problems associated with it. As you help your prospect calculate the Impact of your solution, you need to count these situations, which are related to the main problem your prospect is trying to solve. Adding in the cost of delayed shipments due to production line downtime can dramatically increase the cost associated with the downtime. You may even find an additional Victim is the VP Logistics who suffers from the downtime problem as much or more than his manufacturing counterpart.

So do not simply count the cost of the fundamental problem your solution solves; count the cost of the whole problem; that's true Impact.

Objection Handling

Sometimes the prospect is resistant to your attempting to factor the cost of the problem that your solution removes. Understand that they do not deal with these types of factors every day, that's your job. So when they object have a method for dealing with that quickly, cleanly and fairly.

There's no way to tell what the cost is.

- ✓ "Can I ask you a question?"

OK.

- ✓ "When you say 'there's no way' are you open to a way to assess the cost, if I could show you one?"

Sure.

- ✓ "We have an assessment—an Audit, really—which can help our customers determine the cost of the whole problem and better understand what our solution ultimately will do for them."

Interesting.

- ✓ "Should we talk about scheduling that as a next step?"

Remember

Impact is the COST of the problem, not just the problem itself. This is a *critical* distinction.

Chapter 24: Economics

What is Economics?

The CLIENT™ Economics category addresses those issues related to the process of allocating money to buy your solution, including the people, the requisition paper path and return on investment (ROI.)

Overview

Economics is about how money moves in your prospect's organization to solve problems. Economics deals with funding, Return on Investment, Paper Path, and requisition procedure.

Many sales transactions can be stalled or derailed entirely by the salespersons lack of knowledge of how money moves in the organization to solve problems.

You need to realize that in order to buy your solution, the prospect may be severely challenged by his own organization when he goes and tries to purchase. Understanding this fact will help you to relate to your prospect in ways most salespeople never do and will help you gain additional credibility with your prospect.

Key Economics Questions

Some questions you may want to consider using for the Economics category.

- ✓ "How does money move to solve problems here?"
  - "Easy or difficult?"
  - "Why?"
- ✓ "What kind of Return does the company want to see for large investments?"
- ✓ "Are the problems we're ready to solve big enough to warrant spending money on them?"
  - "Who has the company appointed to inspect and authorize purchase decisions?"
- ✓ "How does the process of requisition work here?
  - "Who starts the requisition process?"
  - "Who finishes the requisition process?"
- ✓ "What happens when someone needs funding to solve a problem?"
  - "What do they have to do to secure funding?"
  - "Who has to approve it?"
- ✓ "How do you fund projects that have not already been budgeted for the year?"
- ✓ "It's important that you make money with—not just spend it on—my solution;"
  - "How do we ensure that happens?"
  - "How do we make it clear in advance?"

Key Economics Tool: The Paper Path

You can learn a lot about your prospect and the buying environment if you can get him to tell you about the Paper Path. The Paper Path is the path the requisition paper travels on its way to approval. From the beginning to the end of the requisition process there are decision makers who must sign off on any large purchase. Understanding who these people are and what they want to see in your eventual proposal to be able to support the purchase is essential information.

There is no such thing as a rubber stamp approval.

You will often find that there are decision makers whom you have not met and who have not given any visible input into the solution requirements. Their opinion is hidden from you until they need to sign or decline. While you may never meet them, or need to, having the Paper Path documented allows you to direct questions to your prospect which will help him with these decision makers when the time comes.

The best way to go about getting the prospect to share this information with you is to simply ask him for it;

- ✓ "Would you mind stepping me through the requisition process?"
- ✓ "How does the process of requisition work here?
    - o "Who starts the requisition process?"
    - o "Who finishes the requisition process?"

Paper Path Different from an Org Chart

The Paper Path is different than the Org chart. While the Org Chart shows you the basic outline of authority and chain of command in the company, the Paper Path will show you all who are involved in actually approving any solution you present for purchase.

Certainly, if you have constructed an Org chart, use it in the Paper Path discussion to help your prospect step you through the process and so you can ask good questions about who is involved and what their stake may be.

ROI

If you have done a good job with Impact, you should be able to get the prospect to share with you the costs and savings that the implementation of your solution will provide their company.

In this case, you can do an excellent job in forecasting ROI or return on investment, for your solution. While some salespeople take the time to offer all kinds of NPV, IRR, etc. related to their ROI, you want to avoid that unless it is your own CFO who is going to present it. Even then, you need to be careful because the prospect simply may not use the same numbers in his business. That will put your ROI in the position of being unnecessarily doubted, which will not be the case if you stick to forecasting a return based on the obvious savings which the core capabilities of your solution will provide.

In other words, if the solution saves downtime of $100,000 per month plus a host of related costs, show those—do not build financial analysis implications on top of them and you will be able to keep yourself squarely in the position of expert and not that of a salesperson that seems to have overreached.

Too Expensive

When the prospect claims you are too expensive, they have taken their focus away from the potential return of the solution and put it on price. This is a common tactic of professional purchasing people. However, salespeople that do not develop an ROI in the first place do not have an excuse when their prospect goes here by default.

If you have developed an ROI, you need to move the prospect's focus back towards it when the "too expensive" issue arises.

You're really too expensive.

✓ "Do you mind if I ask you a question?"

Sure.

✓ "When you say I'm too expensive how do you mean that?"

I don't know if we have the budget for your pricing.

✓ "Mr. Big suggested that you could justify additional budget from the money saved in downtime. Isn't the solution projected to deliver $100,000 per month in savings?"

Well, yes, we hope so.

✓ "But you don't think so? Those numbers were based on what you told me about the cost of downtime in your environment. Did I make a mistake?"

No—they're correct.

✓ "Where are we off? Cutting the price is only adding 1% to your ROI, which is already at 300%. Am I off?"

No, you're on. Look, the purchasing group is behind this and I just needed to ask if you could do anything on the price.

✓ "So, we're good?"

We're good.

In the above example, the salesperson led the prospect to the point where he revealed the truth behind the objection. This is a real life example! When you take the time to patiently ask value added questions you will be in a new position of power and respect with your prospects.

Chapter 25: **Need**

What is the Need?

The CLIENT™ Need category is all about the manner in which the customer will rationalize his decision. Salespeople need to bring objectivity and visibility to the WAY the prospect will make his decision. The prospect can have a problem and still not have a need for your solution.

Uses of Need

Working the CLIENT™ Need category is about ensuring decision integrity. How is the prospect going to make a decision, and how are they going to know that they made the best decision? What things are they going to look at, what requirements and what evidence are they going to have to rely upon to know that they made a good decision?

Be Your Prospect's Decision Advocate

You should take the lead in ensuring that the decision process they are following is the most rigorous, demanding and therefore the best that the prospect could follow to verifiably making the Best Decision Possible.

Become the Monopoly Provider

Establish your solution's key elements (features and benefits) as requirements that any solution they choose should have. Expose your solution as being the only one to fully satisfy the most important aspects of the customer decision.

Get three quotes

Be so well established in your proof of being the best value that when they fulfill what is often a corporate mandate and go to three competitors for quotes that it only HELPS you.

Decision Integrity

The reason why it is so important for the salesperson to understand these issues is because so many prospects are being pulled in all different kinds of directions. They will not always remember or feel the need to remember what they might have said was a good idea when they were in a meeting with you, their salesperson. They might not remember that they agreed to test two competitive solutions under identical conditions.

They might be pressured to make an emotional decision based on whom they like better or who works more comfortably with them. And while this is fine for the salesperson that is winning the deal, if you are not that winning salesperson you might not feel so fine about it.

To be a true asset to your prospect you will protect the integrity of his decision by helping him to see the value of documenting that decision. Once you have helped him understand that, you'll help him to see the value of documenting your solution's features as requirements for the decision. So if you sell a solution whose key feature involves 'process speed,' you'll want to agree that documenting the best decision possible is the right thing to do; and subsequently that the best decision possible would include a solution which had superior 'process speed.'

This way you are providing the prospect with a comfortable and logical authentication path, a path that can lead to your solution being chosen as the only logical choice. Conversely, the same process could lead the prospect, or you, to conclude that yours is not the best solution and to realize this before too much time is wasted. While the fact that you're working to preserve decision integrity does not by default mean that your solution will be chosen, it does mean that your solution--if it is the best for that prospect--will be all the more likely to be chosen.

Prevent Jury-Rigging

The prospect can have a problem you can solve and a great ROI for your solution; but if they judge these things less important than the 'proven' status of the incumbent, for instance, you still lose. The prospect may say all the right things, put you and your solution through the wringer, then make his decision behind closed doors and base that decision on issues either that you were not aware of or that clearly favored another vendor.

Why Would a Prospect Do This?

Why would a prospect spend all that time meeting with you and appear to consider you fairly if he never intended to buy from you? There are many reasons, but chief among them is so that the prospect will appear within his own organization to have done his job.

Often his own company will have strict guidelines to ensure decision integrity and to prevent the prospect from spending company money on a purchase which is not the best solution for the company, but is instead a means for the prospect to make his own job easier or continue courting favor with one vendor or in some way making the decision based on his own personal reasons rather than that of the company as a whole.

If he can manipulate you to deliver a proposal to him, he can later use it to represent to his management that he made a 'fair' decision. This is of great value to him if he has a pre-disposition to your competitor's solution.

Additionally, the prospect is not always so premeditated in his decision. The prospect can also be swayed by influences that drive the prospect to buy something other than the best solution to his problem. In these common instances, the solution to the problem turns out to be a waste of money or worse, as the original problem is left either incompletely solved or unsolved altogether.

Qualify Completely

It is your responsibility to use the tools at your disposal to be sure you have correctly qualified your prospect prior to continuing to invest your own company's time and money attempting to sell to that prospect. And so that the prospect is guided to the best decision possible. This is why there are six areas of qualification in the CLIENT™ qualification index.

Why Document the Decision?

There are several good reasons why both you and the prospect should want to document the Specification Rules.

- ✓ Allows for externalizing the decision
    - o Make the decision objective
- ✓ Makes requirements visible and therefore inspect-able
- ✓ Accountability

    - Hold prospects accountable to fair test vs. incumbent
- ✓ You can influence what goes into the test
    - Now you can negotiate terms of the decision vs. be victimized by them

CLIENT™ Need Questions

Use these Need questions to protect decision integrity.

- ✓ "Is it important to you to make the best decision possible?"
    - "How will you know you've made the best decision possible?"
- ✓ "What evidence will you look at to KNOW that you've made the best decision possible?"
    - "What will you use to determine a fair comparison?"
- ✓ "If the solution failed,
    - "Would there be anyone in particular concerned with how you made the decision?"
    - "What would you want to be able to offer as evidence that it was the best decision possible?"
- ✓ "Can you see any reason why documenting this decision would not be a good idea?"
    - "Would you be open to my assistance in helping put all competitors through a rigorous, fair test?"

Key Tool: Proof Statements

Proof statements are statements which make a claim about a strategic value your solution provides to the prospect, but do so in a way that makes it more than a claim; it becomes a proof because the way the statement is constructed makes sense to the prospect.

Proof statements can be powerful. They can also be fun to put together. The way you put together proof statements is this; you identify key strategic values that your prospects look for. Then you make a list of all the basic facts of your solution and your company. Finally combine the two in an 'indisputable' proof statement.

Facts and Strategic Value

Facts are things that are indisputable. They are items like the age of your company, size, number of employees, location etc.

Strategic value is things like Excellent Service, Responsiveness, Reliability, Stability, Longevity, Assurance, Safest, and Best.

Every salesperson worth the name is capable of whipping out claims as to the strategic value his solution is sure to bring the prospect. But few salespeople 'prove' that the strategic value is sure to be forthcoming. You can do this by making a claim as to strategic value and linking it to a fact. For instance, stating your company is the most reliable solution for the prospect to choose is one thing; saying that your company is the most reliable because of the $12,000,000 cash reserves you maintain is another.

For instance, "highly responsive" is an important strategic attribute your prospects want. Suppose that you work for a small entrepreneurial company. There is no real way for the prospect to know that you are "highly responsive" until he has experienced it himself. In this instance, your proof statement would combine your claim that you are 'highly responsive' with 'evidence.' Compare the following two statements:

- ✓ "My company is highly responsive."

- ✓ "We are a small, entrepreneurial organization which makes us especially suited to providing you with highly responsive service."

The second statement is highly superior and far more impressive. It is more difficult to psychologically challenge than is the first statement, which is a claim that stands by itself, alone.

Competition-Kickers

Competition kickers are negative proof statements directed at your competition. Here you link facts with strategic liability.

For example;

- ✓ "I am not sure how the competition's recent failure at XYZ Corporation will enable you to feel confident as to their claims of the best service, do you?"
- ✓ "I do not know how their downsizing due to financial difficulties will enable you to meet your requirements of a reliable, stable partner for this solution, do you?"
- ✓ "I cannot figure out how their consistent inability to meet delivery times at ABC Company will enable you to feel confident in their ability to meet your service time tables without interruption, do you?"

Remember

The prospect can have a problem and still not have a need for your solution.

Chapter 26: **TimeLine**

What is the TimeLine?

The CLIENT™ TimeLine is the timing of projects and events related to the prospect's business combined with the timing of events on your sales cycle.

Compelling Events

Compelling events are upcoming occurrences that can have a big impact on your ability to sell the prospect a solution. A Compelling Event can either help your sale or hurt it.

Overview

The timeline is a sequential step-by-step layout of the events of your sales cycle leading up to the acquisition of your solution.

Optimally, this information is shared with your prospect. That way, they can help you by pointing out what they're not going to be able to do by a certain date and what they might be able to do by a certain date.

They will also educate you as to situations that might be arising on their own internal timeline that will prevent them from giving full attention to your sales cycle.

Understanding your prospect's Timeline is vital to conducting a successful sales process with them. Knowing when they will be making their decision is essential to positioning your resources and arranging your sales process to put yourself in a position to win.

Personal Story

The first time that I used a timeline, I made a rough sketch of one on a piece of paper and—wincing—I showed it to my prospect who immediately objected.

"I can't commit to that!" he exclaimed pointing to a date when his organization would need to cut their purchase order. I knew it, I said to myself. "Why not?" I asked him.

"Because the actual cutting of the order is done by my boss's boss; it'll be up to him as to whether he can cut it on Friday or the following Monday. I can only commit to getting the requisition and justification sent up by that date, but that's it."

In other words, my first use of a timeline was an outstanding success.

Key Questions

The following key questions will help you articulate a mutually acceptable TimeLine.

- ✓ "What major event is coming in your own industry which your company is getting ready to deal with?"

- ✓ "Are there other significant issues which your company is planning projects to prepare for?"
- ✓ "What are the big projects in your department and when are they slated to conclude?"
- ✓ "Why is the timing of the key projects in your department scheduled the way they are? What events or initiatives drive that?"
- ✓ "Why are your key projects scheduled the way they are? How was the decision to arrange them on their current timeline arrived at?"
- ✓ "Here is the way that we schedule events in our sales process. Does that work for you?"
- ✓ "How fast does the requisition process move here?"
- ✓ "When do you need to start an implementation of a solution by? Why that time?"

Testing the TimeLine

- ✓ "Is there any urgency in getting this proposal to you before next week?"

Yes, definitely.

- ✓ "Really? Why?"

Because the Project personnel have to be in place and productive by June.

- ✓ "What happens if they're not ready by then?"

We lose the whole project and the company may go out of business.

- ✓ "So you need that proposal this week."

Please.

Looking for Compelling Events

Some TimeLine questions you can use to specifically find compelling events.

- ✓ "What major event is coming in your own industry your company is getting ready to deal with?"
- ✓ "Are there other significant issues which your company is planning projects to prepare for?"
- ✓ "What are the big projects in your department and when are they slated to conclude?"

Remember

The timeline is a sequential step by step layout of the events of your sales cycle leading up to the acquisition of your solution; it is more than simply the date the prospect throws out for having the decision made.

Part VII: Sales Process

Chapter 27: About the Sales Process

What is a Sales Process?

The sales process is the sequential series of stages that you guide your sales cycle through on the way to completion.

Sales Cycle vs. Sales Process

A sales cycle is the group of meetings or events that a prospect goes through on the way to buying something.

A sales process on the other hand is a logical course of action imposed on the sales cycle to make it yield either a sale or a quickly disqualified prospect.

A sales process is to a sales cycle what a football team's strategy is to a playoff game.

Benefits of a Sales Process

Pace Yourself

With a sales process you can pace yourself and deploy your own time and resources on a predictable, highly optimized schedule. No more rushing to a proposal which sits on the prospect's shelf or worse, qualifies out your solution in the prospects mind and causes you to lose unnecessarily and before you really had a chance to compete.

Create Momentum

A well designed and properly executed sales process allows you to build momentum with your prospect. Starting the process with correct positioning, and kicking off the discussion with a commanding presentation of information creates a slipstream of momentum which a *true* prospect cannot help but be caught up in.

Manage the customer

A deliberate, focused sales process will match the intuitive manner in which the business prospect makes decisions. So it will help the salesperson greatly in managing the prospect along this predictable, logical and preferred path to the decision.

Tracking

A good sales process means you will be able to track multiple sales processes simultaneously, accurately and with a greatly reduced investment in administrative time to do so. Meaning you will be able to follow a prospect through the sales process and keep on top of the type and quantity of work you need to do to keep the sale progressing, instead of having to stop, collect your notes and thoughts, get with your team, and try to figure it all out every two weeks.

Be Objective in Times of Trouble

When the account or opportunity ceases its smooth movement through your sales process you will be able to be objective in determining why and therefore in getting it moving again. So when they inevitably do not return your phone call or email or just drop off your sales radar for a bit longer than you are comfortable with, you will know it and be able to chart a course to bring it back online.

Be Objective in Looking at the Sum Total of the Business Potential in Your Pipeline

You will be able to look at the sum total of business in your pipeline realistically instead of based on false hope. You will be able to segment your opportunities by stages and by length of time in your sales process.

Improve on Specific Areas of Your Sales Process and Therefore on Specific Areas of Your Sales Effectiveness

How can you improve your sales effectiveness if you cannot tell where in your process you run into trouble and the reason you cannot is because you actually do not have a process in the first place? Yet many salespeople try to improve their effectiveness nonetheless using ineffective spot training or tedious volumes of technical information.

With a sales process you will be able to focus on improving specific areas of your effectiveness by allowing the process to educate you. Where are you having trouble converting from one stage to the next? Is it a sufficient bottleneck that you should drill down and find out why? Perhaps you find that what you are doing in that stage is ineffective; either the information you are presenting is off, the way you are presenting is off, or the people to whom you are presenting it is off. By correcting the issue you can move far more opportunities past that stage and on to closure.

The MAJOR™ Sales Process Overview

The ScoreSelling™ sales process is called MAJOR™. Each letter stands for each of five stages in the process. The first one is M for Momentum; the second one is A for Audit;

the third one is J for Justify; the fourth one is O for Offer; and the fifth and final step is R for Revenue. A brief description of each is as follows.

- ✓ Momentum. The first meeting is called the Momentum stage. In it you see the prospect for the first time, or at least for the first time in this sales cycle. It's termed the Momentum stage because momentum is what you're building.
- ✓ Audit. Here is the step where you meet with the prospect to review his current ways of doing things. You ask lots of relevant CLIENT™ questions in order to form the business case.
- ✓ Justify. You present the business case.
- ✓ Offer. Here you prove your claims usually by means of a proposal. Some solutions require a test or demonstration.
- ✓ Revenue. Terms and conditions, contracts and pricing are finalized here. This is the step when the opportunity is closed.

Chapter 28: **The Pre-Call**

About the Pre-Call

What Is It?

A Pre-Call is a phone conversation with your prospect that is held prior to meeting for the appointment. The Pre-Call is a powerful way to help you prepare for the appointment.

Why Have One?

The Pre-Call lets you get some background information from your prospect. This gives you a reference point for your discussions when you meet face to face.

If significant travel is involved, never go without this step first. You don't want any surprises that would negate the value of the trip.

The Pre-Call is a Phone Call

The Pre-Call is a phone call with the prospect that lasts for about 10-12 minutes. The best time to set the Pre-Call is when you are already on the phone setting up the appointment. Ask if you can ask a few questions so that you can be better prepared when you show up. If he doesn't have the time at that point, schedule a time a few days prior to your meeting.

Ways to Ask for the Pre-Call

- ✓ "Is it OK if I am fully prepared to deliver maximum value to you? I'd just need a few minutes by phone, either now, or at a better time prior to showing up. Can we do that?"

Or,

- ✓ "Would you help me make the most of this upcoming time with you?"

Yes, I suppose.

- ✓ "Would you take a call from me next week to briefly review the meeting agenda and allow me to incorporate any changes before I show up? Takes about 7-11 minutes."

Conducting the Pre-Call

Use CLIENT™ as a way to prepare a few questions for the prospect.

Commitment

Confirm how much time he has available so you can time your discussion appropriately.

- ✓ "Hi John. Thanks for taking the time. Are you OK for 10-15 minutes?"

Yes.

- ✓ "Great. Now when I come and give this presentation, it helps if I can make some examples, based on your own situation. And I appreciate your giving me a chance to be prepared for that."

Sure, go ahead.

Leadership

"Before I begin, can I ask you;"

- ✓ "How did you get started in the business/profession?"
- ✓ "What's an average day look like for you?"
- ✓ "One of the things that scares me is how competitive everything is today and how fast things can change; how do you deal with that?"
- ✓ "What's it going to be like for you about this time next year?"

Impact

Uncover his challenges.

- ✓ "What's one of the biggest challenges you see yourself having to tackle to make that happen?"
- ✓ "What's happening around there lately that made it seem a good use of time to meet with me?"
- ✓ "Any major problems or initiatives you've tackled recently?"

Economics

Feeling for Budget.

- ✓ "I've been hearing that trying to get projects or solutions funded--in general--is like pulling teeth; how do you see it?"
- ✓ "When you folks see a major problem that needs fixing, how does the money move to solve that problem--easily, or with difficulty?"
- ✓ "What's an example of that?"

- ✓ "What kind of ROI do you like to see?"

Need

Touch on the Specification Rules.

- ✓ "What kinds of evidence do you set up to show that you made the best decision possible?"
- ✓ "What do you look at to be sure the ROI/Decision is correct?"
- ✓ "RFP, RFI, RFQ?"

Or,

- ✓ "What do you like to see in order to feel confident overall about making the right decision?"

TimeLine

Find Compelling Events

- ✓ "Any major initiatives you've tackled recently?
- ✓ "Major events on the roadmap? (Customize for your industry.)

Sample

- ✓ "Is there anything happening or slated to happen in your business over the next 6-12 months that you're busy getting ready for?"

Meeting Minutiae

Be sure to get the information about getting to the meeting place. Many times salespeople take on faith that their GPS will get them to the meeting. Confirm the address with the prospect personally. Also confirm;

Address confirmed; Security Protocols
Parking & Entrance: Back, Front or Other
Conference/Meeting room
Call whom upon arrival

Many times these details can be overlooked and cause you to be late or miss the meeting entirely.

Close the Pre-Call by Confirming the Upcoming Meeting

- ✓ "Well, John, I really appreciate your taking the time to speak with me."
- ✓ "I look forward to meeting next Thursday at 8 am; is there anything I can keep in mind in the meantime?"

Email

Send a follow up email confirming what you just discussed and what you are going to be doing when you eventually get together.

- ✓ "I look forward to meeting with you tomorrow at 3 PM to talk about ____ and to hear more about ______. Feel free to contact me with any questions in the meantime."

Update

Update your records, especially your CLIENT Map™.

Chapter 29: **Exciting First Meetings**

The MAJOR™ Momentum Stage

What is it

The MAJOR™ Momentum Stage is your First Meeting with the prospect. Your goal is to excite them!

Building Buyer's Equity in the MAJOR™ Momentum Stage

Your mission for building Buyer's Equity (CLIENT™) for your solution in the Momentum step is straightforward and simple; get the Audit. Create urgency to identify and solve problems. You may have heard other salespeople describe a first meeting as being anything from a question and answer session to a seeding opportunity.

It is neither.

It is an opportunity for you to present a compelling business reason for this prospect to take the next step. It is not about making a new friend, establishing a contact, feeling out the opportunity, making an impression. It's not about selling the people, winning their support or getting more informed.

Your sole objective is to get the Audit scheduled. It is about getting in, creating urgency, securing the advance, and getting out. Period. Just get the Audit. Decide later, when you're alone or with your sales team, whether or not the opportunity should be pursued. For now, focus on getting good at securing the Audit.

The First Meeting Test

Do you have an effective First Meeting plan? Most salespeople take the "show up and throw up" posture. Double-check to see if any of these apply to you as the presence of any one poses a real threat to your effectiveness;

- Open Ended Discussion
- Tossing Ideas Around
- Seeing if Things "Stick"
- No Marketing Literature
- No PowerPoint®
- No Materials
- No Script
- No Pre-Defined Next Step

Many salespeople feel that the First Meeting should be an "open-ended" discussion to "ensure the prospect has a need." They feel that presenting information at this stage is "too early" and makes them appear "too salesy." It's hard to argue with the apparent logic in their seemingly veteran comments; but do your best because you will go broke otherwise.

Give yourself a pat on the back if the following applies to you;

- ✓ Compelling information that earns a defined next step.

- ✓ A presentation which describes problems the prospect is experiencing or concerned about;
- ✓ Information that demonstrates the inferiority of competitive or alternative solutions (kicking the competition!)
- ✓ Case reviews, impressive literature and a discussion track.

Your Presentation

Haven't you always wanted to sell a solution that has a huge positive impact on your prospect; something where the incredible superiority of that solution is immediately obvious?

Let's face it; every salesperson wants that. So why don't you have it?

Why, after you present, is the customer not sitting in a daze? Why aren't they fumbling for words, in a state of amazement, stammering out "C-could you show me that again?"

Facts

Well, you say, because my solution just isn't 'like that.' It takes a lot of 'education' of your prospect, to 'get them ready' to 'see the light.' You might sell something like janitorial, or a service solution or a software application that delivers efficiencies to database administrators who are in the middle of a particular platform migration.

There's a lot of solutions that are boring—to laypeople; to the average man on the street. But they're not boring to your prospect, if he is, after all, a prospect. So neither the solution—whatever it might be—nor the prospect is the problem.

So, most salespeople already sell the type of solution that has the huge positive impact; but most salespeople present it in such a way that the impact is obscured. Presenting like that means you live in the world of objections and price-slashing and taking abuse and losing constantly and scratching and clawing to pay your bills.

Most salespeople do not know how to present the impact of their solution with power. Most of them don't even know what that impact is, because most of them never learn what it is about their solution that helps the prospect. Most of them never learn what problem the prospect must have in order for their solution to be a solution.

On the other hand, there are top salespeople that can sell a ream of paper like its greenback paper from the National Mint.

The difference is in the quality of information presented.

Get a Presentation

There can be no more vital a tool in your sales arsenal than a power packed, informative, value-added presentation. One that jolts the prospect and shocks him into a frantic mental scramble to figure out just how he is going to survive without your solution.

By creating a presentation like this, you will immediately set yourself apart from the other sales oriented, baited presentations that are put out by your competition. It will certainly set you apart from the salesperson that shows up with nothing in hand, expecting to be able to question the prospect to death and thereby earn himself a new customer.

Investing in this presentation will provide you with the best opportunity to sell to this prospect. The reason is simple; prospects, as we have discussed, are eager for information, good information, which they can use immediately. Offer it and they will meet with you. Present it and they will buy from you.

So how do you get one of these presentations?

Building the Presentation

First, you've got to get hold of information that your prospect really cares about. If you are completely unfamiliar with your own industry, get familiar. Take the time, make the investment. Get with your sales manager, or a senior salesperson. Meet with your technical people. Meet with your product development people, if you have them. Talk to your company owner if you can, or get a meeting with a knowledgeable executive if you don't. In each discussion, find out what they think the important trends are and why. Ask them how they know their beliefs to be true (be nice about it.) You want to find out what's going on first, and second, if there are sources of information you can access to grow out your expertise.

Pick a few trends and study them out, seeing if there is a direct impact on your industry, on your customer and maybe on the way that your company chooses to serve its customers and how that might help. Remember Y2K? Consider worldwide trends like Globalization, Outsourcing, Competitiveness and Free Trade. Look up information on the emerging economic powers of India, Russia, China and the Eastern European countries.

Now, you're in a position to take the next step; talk to your customers. Pick 3-5 good users of your solution. Schedule a meeting with them, take them to lunch afterwards. Ask for a tour and for permission to get to know what's going on; very few will turn down an opportunity to be the 'resident-expert' for you. Pound them with questions; why did they buy your solution, how does it help them, what keeps them up at night, what's coming down the pike, and so on.

Finally, with your sales team, hammer out 5-7 key trends that are developing in your industry that you can go educate your prospects about. Good examples of this are those things that happen in their business as a result of not having your solution, from your company, and from you personally. Leave nothing out—you'll edit this later. A key way to do this is to 'hollow out' your benefit statements. That is, what does NOT happen as a result of NOT having your solution? What inefficiencies exist and how do these compound other inefficiencies?

Draw implications. What else doesn't happen, completely unrelated to your solution? What other departments might run behind? What happens to overall productivity? To worker morale? Will the company culture be affected? Draw implications on implications. You just might be amazed at where you end up. Again, you're not editing yet, so keep going.

Set up a couple test runs on a spreadsheet and drill into some basic cost analyses. Saving only 20 minutes per day for 5 employees paid an average salary of $37,500 will get you $10,441 in annual Return on Investment. If you sell a $20,000 solution, your customer makes his money back in less than 24 months, and will net an additional $32,207 over five years. You will be blown away as these numbers begin to stack up.

Once you've got a reasonable series of issues and trends that your industry is facing (and it certainly helps to confirm these with an industry expert or think tank and your own management) you're ready to begin assembling your presentation.

Keep it simple. The whole show shouldn't take more than 20-25 minutes. If you're using PowerPoint® keep it under 10-12 slides. Do NOT overload graphics, pretty pictures, backgrounds or sound. Don't wear out your prospect with your complete ineffectiveness in graphic design. DO overwhelm them with your knowledge of your industry. The following format is a helpful guide.

- What Is Happening? Focus, focus, focus on the BAD news. If there is a tsunami headed in their direction, TELL them about it.
- Why it's Different. Why is what is happening today and what is coming down the road so very different from what has always been happening? How is it going to affect them?
- What That Means to Companies in that industry. Has anyone been affected yet? Can you show valid, reasonable parallels from those experiences to the potential impact on the prospect you are talking with? Do so.
- Why You Should Take Action. Do we really need to explain this? If you want to avoid catastrophe, start now. Talk about implementation times and how far ahead they will need to prepare, the average company will need to prepare, in order to be ready to deal with the current and coming challenges.
- Some Possible Courses of Action. Mention some ways they can begin to get ready now. Mention your own company. Since an Audit is most likely your next step, insert an option called 'Expert Quantification' or 'Third Party Industry Analysis' or something like that.

That is the general flow of this information presentation. Again, it doesn't need to be overdone, so commit to it and just get it done.

What will happen as a result of this power packed presentation is two-fold. First your prospects will turn into customers faster and second, you won't be able to wait to give this presentation. You'll be so excited by what you get to talk about and the effect it has on your audience that your job will take on a whole new aspect of fun to it.

The Presentation

The presentation is the key means by which you deliver value to the prospect and build urgency for him to follow your sales process. As you have already seen in the Messaging section, you should have an assembled presentation ready to go for your prospect.

The presentation is a package of concise, compelling information that is going to have an immediate helpful impact on the customer's business. This information is going to speak to the prospect in a way that you, as a sales professional, never could. The presentation of this information will establish you as an expert, faster and more effectively than any other method could. It will allow you to both maintain control of the meeting and deliver your message in a compelling and commanding fashion. This presentation is how you complete the meeting in a minimum of time with a maximum of delivery of value to the prospect.

PowerPoint®

Use PowerPoint® presentations for your prospect. The prospect will always agree to your meeting easier if he believes you have taken time to prepare good information for him. It's an easier proposition for him to accept, providing a minimal time envelope and a maximum of information for that time.

Your benefits as a salesperson are significant. Your prospect in agreeing to letting you give him a presentation is essentially handing over the control of the meeting to you; very good indeed.

You can prepare in advance an impact-drenched impression, wordsmith your claims and practice your presentation to perfection.

You can pre-define the objections you will be getting and destroy those objections before they ever come up.

Presentation Format

The format of your presentation can be as the one used in the Messaging section or the one presented here.

That format is;

- ✓ Who We Are
- ✓ What We Do
- ✓ Why We're Better
- ✓ What Our Customers Say
- ✓ What You'll Get From Us

This format is clean, logical and effective.

Who We Are

Brainstorm the following questions and add information where appropriate.

- ✓ Where and When Company Started, and How
  - o Faced and Overcame Obstacles Like…
- ✓ Current Status

- Employees and Sales
- Customer base numbers

✓ Unique Accomplishments

- 1-2 sentences tops

Sample Who We Are Slide

- Company founded in 1997
  - As a small solutions based company of 3 people
- From that time until today
  - Have grown to a 350 employee, $120 million firm
  - Servicing the Needs of a Distinguished customer base
  - From small startups to Fortune 500
  - With unique and varied demands

What We Do

Brainstorm your solution's benefits and features. Ask the following;

✓ Key Features of Solution

✓ Return on Investment of Solution in which Key Areas

✓ Why Do People Buy Your Solution?

Sample What We Do Slide

- What we do is to provide solutions for those companies which;
  - Drive productivity
  - Reduce costs
  - Increase Profits/Revenue

Why We're Better

Think, think, think!

- ✓ What attributes are unique:
  - Company
  - People
  - Solution
  - Features: Product or Service
- ✓ Patentable?
  - Maybe Not
  - BUT
  - They Can Sound Like it!!

Sample Why We're Better Slide

- We do this by means of two things
  - The first is; ________
    - This is a core competence of our company (or patented product of process)
    - Which allows us to:
  - The second is; _____
    - A unique feature of our solution
    - Which allows us to:
- NO ONE else can offer these!

Sample What Our Customers Say Slide

- Customer A:
- Faced a situation of:
  - They feared:
  - What we did was:
  - This allowed them to:
    - Save $
    - Reduce Cost,

        - Increase their Time to Market
        - Drive Profitability
    - They sum up their experience with us as______.

What You'll Get From Us

- ✓ Convey Longevity
- ✓ Reliability
- ✓ Service
- ✓ Show How Your Company is the Least-Risk Alternative

Sample What You'll Get From Us Slide

- We ensure our continued ability to deliver these results to our customers by:
    - Comprehensive Customer Service (# people, certifications, etc.)
    - Improvement Program / Quality Assurance
    - Ongoing Investments & Financial Stability

Helpful PowerPoint® Hints

To use PowerPoint® effectively you need to know your audience. But some general rules apply as well;

- Keep it Brief and Focus!
    - Know Your Audience
    - No Run-on Text Sentences
- Pictures Sell!
    - Free clipart library at www.microsoft.com
- Keep Formatting Consistent
    - Not too small
    - Standard Theme Colors
    - Standard Placement

Planning the First Meeting

The CLIENT Map™

Your CLIENT Map™ Account Profile will help you to prepare for the meeting.

- ✓ If you use it.

You should be able to complete the Detailed Snapshot on page 3 of the CLIENT Map™; at least take a serious pass at doing so.

Meeting Plan

Using a Meeting Plan starting on page 16 of the CLIENT Map™ will ensure you are fully prepared.

After the Meeting

After the meeting, return to your CLIENT Map™ and fill in the answers.

Holding the First Meeting

A Sample CLIENT™ Discussion Track

Shake hands and introduce yourself and whoever else might be with you. Keep the small talk limited.

Thank the prospect for inviting you in. Confirm the amount of time that he has. You don't want to get halfway through your presentation and suddenly be out of time.

After you have identified how much time he has, briefly review how you got here and describe a reasonable objective for the meeting. If you have an Agenda, present it and step through it concisely. Close for agreement.

It might look like;

- ✓ "John, thank you for inviting us. Before I begin I'd like to make sure that this is still a comfortable time for you to meet?"

Yes, it is.

- ✓ "And I have planned on meeting for about 60 minutes. If we finish early that's fine. Does that still work for you?"

Yes, it does.

Be sure that you know who is at your meeting. If anyone has come in that you do not know, shake their hand, give them a card and thank them for coming. When the time is right, ask your contact for permission for more formal introductions.

- ✓ "John, can we go around the table before we begin and just get a feel for who we all are?"

Finish the roundtable and get into the presentation.

- ✓ "Great, thanks. Why don't we get started, so long as there aren't any questions?"

Deliver the presentation.

Commitment

Do not stop after you deliver the presentation. Flick on the lights, remain standing and start the line of questions. You are looking, first off, to see if they have bought off on the problems you mentioned in your presentation.

Note: if your presentation is weak, you're going to go down fast in this line of questioning. Make sure it doesn't.

Keep refining it. Ask for honest, brutal feedback and stand up and take it and fix it.

Once you have the right presentation in place, DON'T question the veracity. You told the truth. As such, you don't need to coddle, or whine, or beg for the prospects help. You've just told him there's a tsunami coming—you going to get caught up in how comfortable he is while you whisk him to safety? If you are, you're going to signal to him that what you told him really isn't true.

- ✓ "I am really interested in your opinion on what we talked about. What did you think?"
- ✓ "Did any of the problems we discussed resonate with you?"

The prospect may answer one of two ways—either "yes" or "No."

Yes.

- ✓ "Which ones?"
- ✓ "Really, why?"

No.

- ✓ "Really, why?"
- ✓ "What should have been there to make it a better use of your time?"

Leadership

Ask any prepared questions you have about the decision makers, and how they might be affected.

- ✓ "Who does that impact?"
- ✓ "People in this room?"
- ✓ "What is the visibility to that on the Executive level? When I spoke to Mr. Big it seemed to be high."

Impact

Qualify their problem.

- ✓ "How big a problem is it?"
- ✓ "Why? How do you know that?"
- ✓ "What's it costing you?"

Economics

Qualify that funding is available for a solution.

- ✓ "Does money move to solve problems like that; or does it stay bottled up for bigger problems?"
- ✓ "What kind of Return on Investment is needed?"

Need

Explore their Specification Rules.

- ✓ "How would you know if that ROI is valid?"
- ✓ "What kind of proof is needed?"
- ✓ "Are there competitive projects, or would this be the first attempt at fixing it?"

TimeLine

Finally, ensure the timing.

- ✓ "Are there things in the way that would prevent you being able to look at this now? In the near future?"

Qualify the Next Step

Commitment

Move to solidify the next step.

"After what we've been talking about, is there value in quantifying what we can do for you? In showing that, to your comfort level, we could save you $X00's? Or knowing for sure that we cannot?"

I don't know yet. I would need more information first.

"Do you mind if I make a suggestion?"

OK.

"Let's take a preliminary step. We have a document that quantifies our potential value to you based exactly on your own situation and shows you clearly what to expect from our solution. Would there be value in that?"

Why, yes, I suppose so. What do I have to do for that?

"Invest a ½ day, (or a morning, a day, an afternoon, a couple hours) so we could go over some questions. Then, I take the answers, compile them, add our solution and impact areas and present that back to you. You just need to involve whoever you think is going to be a stakeholder in the problem."

OK, I think I could do that.

Leadership

Now, map out who is going to be part of the decision. You want to know the people, who they are, what their stake is and how accessible they will be to this process. Ultimately you want to know the final authority in the decision (Mr. Big) the initial requisition writer (who is probably your contact) and everyone in between.

For your purposes now, though, you want the people that the prospect is comfortably able to get to the meeting. Give him suggestions, based on your own industry and needs.

- ✓ "Would there be anyone else's input beside you?"
- ✓ "Can we talk about whose input you'd want?"
- ✓ "Who ultimately decides?"

✓ "By himself?"

No, he has a number of people in to help him—a team.

✓ "Who does he tap for that team?"

Well, me, actually. I help.

✓ "Anyone else?"

Sure, Bill and Tom.

✓ "Can they be available for our Audit?"

Yes, I think so.

Impact

Confirm the problems you will be examining in the Audit.

- ✓ "Which processes or problems are we going to focus on first?"
- ✓ "Why those?"
- ✓ "OK. And second, in order of importance?"
- ✓ "Third?"
- ✓ "OK. Any others?"

Economics

Ask about budget.

- ✓ "How do projects—which solve these types of problems--get funded?" (By the way, speaking of 'purchases' in terms of 'projects' will take you a long way towards affirming in the prospect that you 'get it' versus some sales guy who is always talking about purchases and decisions.)
- ✓ "If you felt comfortable that you had a solution to those problems, what kinds of challenges will you face in getting a budget for the solution?"

Need

Confirm the way they like to receive information.

- ✓ "We will be documenting this information. Any particular format you'd like that in?"

TimeLine

Pick the date and time.

- ✓ "When does it need to be done?"

Problems and Objections

Problems and objections will come when either you or the prospect is operating under information that is either incomplete or wrong. In these instances, if you feel uncomfortable, move to the next topic in the CLIENT™ sequence, but come back to it later, changing the wording slightly.

Chapter 30: **InterSelling™**

What is InterSelling™?

InterSelling™ is a process of keeping in touch with the prospect between meetings. Using email, phone, voicemail and letters, a logical chain of communication is kicked off at the end of one meeting and continues until just before the next meeting.

What Happens After a "Good Meeting"

Immediately upon leaving the prospect's office, you should operate on the assumption that everything the prospect told you is going to go wrong. Especially today, when the prospect is going to be bombarded with information from all directions on a thousand different issues within hours of leaving your meeting.

This is simply because if the prospect is truly interested in proceeding with you and wants the support of his peers, he will most likely face some internal resistance and will feel a dampening of enthusiasm because of it; there are only so many battles he can fight.

Salespeople on the other hand, feel better and better after leaving a good meeting with the prospect. As their week goes on and tough things happen from other prospects, the salesperson looks back on this good meeting and feels better and better. In his mind the deal is practically closed just as it's begun, and he deludes himself into emotionally believing that everything is going to go as planned. In short, the salesperson gives up control. When the prospect calls back and cancels, the stunned salesperson can only commit to follow up at a later time.

Why Use InterSelling™

InterSelling™ prevents this. With InterSelling™ you keep control by maintaining contact. You keep the prospect involved by not letting him get too distant from you. You deliver a string of communications on schedule, designed to keep your name and information familiar to the prospect. Therefore, you improve the likelihood of either his meeting with you, or his informing you of a problem in enough time for you to do something about it.

InterSelling™ Sample Schedule

A sample InterSelling™ schedule follows.

Thank you note

Use a standard folded 5x8. Put it in the mail before the end of the day on which you had your meeting. Get in the habit of writing these in the car after your meeting, or even before the meeting; then drop them in the mail as soon after your meeting as possible. These will arrive 1-3 days later.

Call back or voicemail

Advise him of how you have begun finding the answer to one or more of his questions. Call before the end of the same day you meet, or as soon as you have begun to find out. Leave him a voicemail that says;

- ✓ "Hi, John; I just wanted to let you know that I spoke to my Director about your specific question; he thought the best thing would be for him to contact corporate and get the full answer. He'll have an answer back to me by tomorrow in the morning. I'll be in touch with you after that. Thanks."

Email

Send the next afternoon or day after. Advise him of the answer to his question and let him know he can have the answer in more detail, or in documentation, or whatever he wants, when you meet to conduct the Audit.

Letter

Send it out 3-4 days later. This will arrive about one week after your meeting and therefore, about one week before your Audit. In the letter, thank him for his time, specify the date and time of the Audit and give a brief agenda over what you will be going over at that time.

Email 2

Send it three days prior to the meeting. Advise him you will be calling him the next day to confirm and answer any last minute questions that might have come up.

Call

2 days prior. Call and do what your email stated. Do NOT go into detail. Just confirm your meeting, ask if there are any other issues, thank him and get off the phone.

Objections and Derails

There are only three things that can happen during the InterSelling™ stage that you need to be concerned with. They are;

- The prospect quits,
- The prospect delays, or
- The prospect keeps going.

If the prospect bails out on you, find out why immediately. If he's set on bailing, let him go. But if you can get another meeting, and you feel it's worth it, go for it. Maybe he just needs more information from you.

Delays are less of an issue, obviously—just try to understand why the delay is occurring and if it bodes well or ill for you. Do NOT try to force this meeting time sooner if he's only requesting a few days delay. Again, if there's weeks or months involved, ask for another meeting, or simply confront the prospect and ask if what he really is doing is cutting things off, and trying to spare your feelings. You want to know what is really happening so you can get on with addressing it.

Remember, your success depends on your ability to keep the prospect on track. If you *don't know* he's off track, that's something you cannot do. And a prospect always derails hours or days before he tells the 'waiting' salesperson. The prospect has all that time to get entrenched with his decision to put you off, and when he does initiate the call, you will face a determined prospect with nothing other than your own surprise and disappointment to counter him; not much of a strategy. However, if you're InterSelling™ you will most likely be able to deal with the prospect before he is set on breaking the commitment with you. Better yet, your InterSelling™ may be the very thing that convicts him to not even consider breaking things off in the first place.

All these communications may seem like a lot of work to you. Don't make them broken record redundancies. But as for the work required from you—there are lots of tools available today that make this easier. You can create a letter template and a format for writing the thank you note. Even so, it will still be more work than the typical "waiting" strategy with which the average salesperson passes the time between prospect visits; but then again, do you really want anything that the average salesperson gets?

Chapter 31: The Audit

What is the MAJOR™ Audit Stage?

The MAJOR™ Audit Stage is a meeting designed to do one thing; supply you with an interested and cooperative prospect to answer all the questions you need to know to sell them.

It is a follow up to the First Meeting—the MAJOR™ Momentum Stage—and is usually an extended meeting, from one to four hours.

What the Audit is Not

The Audit is not about preparing a proposal for the prospect. This is very important. You are not preparing a proposal for the prospect, but conducting an analysis that will deliver a business case, which may include one or more options to proceed.

In the presentation of the business case (which is the next stage of the MAJOR™ Sales process—the Justify stage) you will present these options for proceeding. The prospect will choose the option they prefer, you will qualify their choice, *and then* you will prepare a proposal and present it (in the MAJOR™ Offer Stage.)

Each stage of the MAJOR™ Sales Process serves an important and unique purpose.

Why No Proposal Yet?

When the prospect receives a proposal from you, he rightly concludes you are finished and that it is now up to him to decide what to do, if anything. Additionally, the prospect may try to persuade you to "just send" the proposal to him and let him read it in his own time. And how will you avoid doing that—by blatant refusal?

You do not want any expectation of a proposal coming as an outcome of this Audit meeting, since this will limit your ability to get back in the account and sell.

How Do You Get an Audit?

You are able to secure this meeting because of your excellence in the MAJOR™ Momentum Stage. Your presentation was so compelling and your expertise so evident the prospect is ready to give you the information you need to demonstrate how effective your solution could be for them; they rightly consider your offer to show them what your solution can do for them as an instant value proposition.

Building Buyer's Equity (CLIENT™) in the MAJOR™ Audit Stage

You can build significant Buyer's Equity for your solution simply by conducting an Audit in the first place. Very few sales professionals express any concern for the need to truly understand their prospect's business environment and challenges, let alone spend half of your day learning about them. Your conduct should be one of an expert; be a careful listener and an asker of good questions.

For Example

Been to the Doctor's office lately? Maybe you've had to meet with your attorney (so sorry.) What about your Financial Advisor? Maybe you've had to take the car in for service?

All the above are examples where you probably experienced an expert asking you questions. Questions that were designed to help an expert properly characterize a problem so he could make a recommendation as to a solution to it. When your Doctor or Attorney or even your Mechanic made the recommendation, you more readily agreed to it, even if you didn't like the price.

How many salespeople sell like that?

Before you say it won't work for your industry you'll need to give it a chance because you can bet dollars to donuts that's exactly the way the big-ticket sales are made in your industry since that's the way the high dollar sales are made in *every* industry.

Sample Audit Agenda

A sample Audit Agenda might include the following;

- Introductions
- Questionnaire
- Problem Identification
- Current Method Review
- Process Mapping
- Need to Change
- Assess Cost of Current Method
- Implications of Current Method
- Projected Cost to Change

Your role in the Audit is to be the expert who asks the questions; you are never the salesperson pushing solutions (at least not yet.)

Need to Know (N2K)

The Need to Know list is essential to an effective Audit. The N2K list will provide you with a reference to consult for qualifying the prospect, both from a sales perspective (CLIENT™) and also from a technical perspective.

Technical Need to Know (N2K)

Your company probably provides some form of documentation for "needs analysis." Questions are usually limited to the technical specifications surrounding the solution recommendation. They tend to be focused on what you need to know for the implementation or actual delivery of the solution. Use this document to generate those questions you need to deliver a good business case.

Sales Need to Know (N2K)

Your sales Need to Know list is the CLIENT™ items in your CLIENT Map™ (CLIENT MAJOR™ Account Profile.) The CLIENT Map™ contains questions that constitute a qualified prospect for your solution.

- How willing are they to change?
- Who ultimately makes the decision?
- What is the size of the current problem?
- What is the problem's cost?
- How will they make their decision?
- When will they make their decision?

Your Audit Document

Use your N2K list to create a document for conducting your Audit.

What Your Audit Document Will Do For You

Your Audit document will be a formal document that you will use to guide the prospect through the Audit. This will help keep you on track as you conduct the Audit and limit distractions.

Additionally, it will serve the important purpose of reaffirming to your prospect that this Audit is an authentic step in the process, not merely a poorly staged excuse to wrench sales information from him.

Finally, the document will allow you to easily re-purpose or transition to creating a business case for the MAJOR™ Justify Stage.

Planning the Audit

Much good will comes of taking the time to thoroughly plan out the Audit step. Use the available ScoreSelling™ tools for your Audit meeting.

CLIENT Map™

Before the meeting, conduct a strategy session both by yourself and with your team, including your Sales Manager. Spend time on each of the CLIENT™ issues you want to know more of. Compile a list of questions and an agenda for the meeting.

Meeting Plan

Using a Meeting Plan starting on page 17 of the CLIENT Map™ will ensure you are fully prepared.

After the Meeting

After the meeting, return to your CLIENT Map™ and fill in the answers.

A Sample CLIENT™ Discussion Track

The purpose of showing a discussion track is that you see the use of the various CLIENT™ qualifying questions. Use this as a learning tool to construct your own, while understanding that no script will ever be followed exactly as it is written, but will serve as a valuable tool in preparing you for your selling situations. This script as shown here is not meant to be copied and pasted; it is rather meant to be adapted as you see fit.

The Audit Outcome

Set the outcome first. You want information that will help you to establish a business case and come back with one or more options and the value of each.

Remember, this is not about generating a proposal!

Commitment

Open by thanking your prospect for meeting. Confirm the amount of time that they have to work with you. As part of your preparing of the prospect, you would have told him that you wished to take him to lunch or have lunch brought in. The thing is lunch is an important step and puts them in a position where they can relax a bit.

- ✓ "Thanks for having me in today. I look forward to our discussion and learning more about your operation."
- ✓ "As we discussed, this meeting should take us about two hours. We're here to ask a number of questions which will comprise the basis of our assessment; after which I will be able to construct a scenario with some options and bring that back to you at some point over the next couple weeks."

- ✓ "When I come back, I will NOT be bringing a proposal, but will have some options which can serve as the basis for a future proposal, should you decide you want one. Does that sound fair?"

Yes.

- ✓ "Good. Also, given the time we will be spending here, I'd like to invite you to lunch afterwards if you are able to join me."

That sounds great.

- ✓ "Any questions at this point?"

Leadership

Ensure that they have all the people available you need. If someone cannot be there, find out whom. Ask your contact, (who may be your Campaigner by now) when will that person be available; or if they would be available for a phone call from you. Do not simply strike them off the list. Their input may have a huge impact on your sale.

Fill out the CLIENT™ Organizational chart (page 6 of the CLIENT Map™.) Start by asking for one of their own; if they don't want to give you one, begin filling out the one you have. Ask for specific input on relationships, roles and responsibilities, and power structure. Be sure about titles. Ask if you have the correct spelling of names. Do not skimp on this part. If there's someone appearing on the power structure that is not in the meeting room, ask the prospect if they will be available at a later time.

Impact

Identify in as much detail as possible how they're doing business without your solution now. Drill down on the process(es) that you are going to need to improve.

Even if your solution allows them to do something they were not able to do before, there has to be some processes that are being replaced. Document those.

- ✓ "How do you do that now?" Drill down. Asking "why?"
- ✓ "How big a problem is that?"
- ✓ "How do you mean that?"
- ✓ "How do you know it's that big?"
- ✓ "What does that cost?"
- ✓ "Who knows about that?"
- ✓ "Who cares about that?"

Economics

Ask about the level of Return on Investment that they will need to get forward momentum. Confirm it again.

- ✓ "What's the pie-in-the sky ROI you'd love to see to justify a business case?"
- ✓ "Is that realistic or attainable here?"
- ✓ "What's the minimum level of return you need to see to go forward on similar projects?"

Need

Qualify the manner in which they will be making any decision.

- ✓ "Is it important to you to make the best decision possible?"
- ✓ "How will you know you've made the best decision possible?"

✓ "What evidence will you look at to know that you've made the best decision possible?"

Qualify the type of proof they consider to validate a good decision; things like customer references, exact case studies or simply a well designed proposal.

TimeLine

✓ "So, is there value in having proof that this ROI is real, or not?"

Yes, definitely.

✓ "Is there value in having that proof sooner rather than later?"

Well, yes. Especially if it's going to save a lot. We need to know that sooner rather than later.

Sample of Active Sales Questions

Commitment

"Then, if I were to put the resources into providing that proof, would you be able to just be sure of one thing? That if you wanted to, there is nothing to prohibit you from making a decision on it within the time period?"

I don't know if we're going to be able to buy it; I don't know if I even want to yet.

"I don't want you to buy it yet; I want to you to find out if there is anything prohibiting you from buying it yet."

I'm not sure what that means.

"It means that, if you had proof of its value and you wanted to get it, that you could get it. That there's nothing preventing you from doing that."

I see. I just need to make sure that there's nothing on the corporate agenda that's keeping us from buying, if we want something?

"Right."

That's fair. I'll talk to my CEO.

"Can you get him to the next meeting?"

That's not a bad idea; then it's you presenting, not me.

"Exactly."

I'll check. Could you grease the sled by sending him an invitation?

Get commitment for your highest Executive contact to be at the next meeting, the Justify meeting. His presence there will take weeks off of your sales process.

Leadership

Start by identifying who is going to be at the Justify meeting. Find out exactly who they're going to be. Be sure to ask for specific personnel to be there.

Management doesn't like it when they're asked to make a decision on something they didn't know about until you brought it up. Ask them in advance, that way they can weigh in and tell you what else needs to be there.

Also, confirm that your Campaigner is going to support the information he just gave you when he is in front of Mr. Big.

Impact

Hone down and confirm the top three problems; the ones that are going to provide 80% of the Return on Investment for your solution.

Economics

Ask questions on the paper path. Pull out your organizational chart and ask;

- ✓ "How does the requisition get approved internally here?"
- ✓ "How long does it take to do that?"

Ask the prospect to be as specific as possible. Do not be put off, but don't be overaggressive either. You want to understand how things work; what kind of challenges they are going to face if they decide to move forward on your solution.

- ✓ "Can I ask you about the ROI for a second?"
- ✓ "When you do buy, who starts the requisition process?"
- ✓ "And where does it go from there?"

For each person ask; "What do they want to see to give it a yes?"

- ✓ "Why will they say no?"

Need

Identify any "pie in the sky" requirements. Ask them to identify their wish list of capabilities in addressing these problems.

- ✓ "I can't make any promises; but what else would you want to see in order to be sure it was right for you?"

Find out what else they're looking at competitively;

- ✓ "Everyone today needs to feel they've checked other options; who else are you considering in this decision?"
- ✓ "There's usually someone who thinks that there's a different direction to go in solving this; what else are you considering from a solution perspective?"

TimeLine

Confirm the date for the meeting. Also, find out whether or not anything has come up on the company timeline that might impact their ability to implement a decision in the foreseeable future.

Problems and Objections

Refusal to share information with you is the biggest problem you will face. Although it is true that a prospect will rarely agree to see you for an Audit and simultaneously refuse to share information with you. But what often happens is they do not want to share information with you that they think you do not need. Simply explain that you need the information and confirm what it is you are going to use it for. If they still refuse, you can handle it in one of two ways.

If the Information is Vital to You.

"John, I understand that you don't want to share that information with me. I am not sure why?"

Well, it doesn't seem to be necessary to telling me how you are going to help me.

"I see. I don't know what to do about that. You see, that information is important to the process. As a matter of fact, if

I don't have it, I can't make heads or tails of what's going on here. Can I make a suggestion?"

Sure.

"Can I show you how we intend to use it? And then you can let me know, after I talk about that, if in that light, you can work with me on it, or offer me some other suggestion, or maybe just let me know that we shouldn't proceed. Is that fair?"

Yes, that sounds OK.

"Great. Here's where it fits in …"

The real thing that you're doing here is letting the prospect cool off and giving him some time to save face as you demonstrate your reasonable, professional approach to his problem. If, in the end, he still won't budge, you need to exit. Do so graciously. After all, you cannot do anything without the information, right? See 'Bailing Out' below.

If the Information is Not Vital

If the information isn't vital, you've got more flexibility, obviously. But you still need to handle it delicately. If you just stepped into something where he is really threatened, you cannot simply cheerily step back and move on to another area. Again, confirm why you wanted to know about it, ask why he doesn't want to talk about that, ensure he is comfortable with things and move on smoothly.

Bailing Out

If the prospect says that they are not willing to confirm if anything prevents them from purchasing, but they still want to test your solution or get a proposal from you, you have a choice to make. Most often, the situation is not going result in a sale for you. The prospect is going to evaluate you and make a decision without cooperating with your requests for more information. So, you need to decide if your time is better spent selling to someone who is more cooperative. And bailing out on this prospect may give you an opportunity to sell to them again at a later time. Just make sure that you do it politely, with grace.

The common cause of this type of behavior on the part of the prospect is that he has already made a decision and does not want to let you know about it. In that case, the other option open to you is to call on Mr. Big yourself and explain the situation. If you have already spoken to him, and if he has already been a part of the discussions prior to this point, you may be able to get him involved and get things on track again.

One final note about resistance; sometimes you're just talking to someone who is way too low on the totem pole. If your contact is too low on the organizational chart, he will absolutely freak out at the notion of asking questions of his executives about purchase decisions. If you have taken the proper steps in your prospecting, this won't happen; but if you have not, it might. Watch out for it.

Ways to Handle Resistance

"Do you want this test to be conclusive, or do you want to do it all again at some later point in time?"

Well, I want it to be conclusive.

"Then, I suggest that we get the people who want to give input, to give input up front."

But that's what we're doing.

"Not quite. Because if you tried to buy it, are there people who can stop you? Who can say no and request more information?"

Well, yes.

"In that case what happens?"

Well, we have to incorporate their requests.

"And re-write the proposal?"

If necessary, yes.

"Then, doesn't it make sense to ask them to tell us up front what they will approve? And get their feedback now, rather than guess and hope we have it right when we do the test?"

I see what you are saying.

"OK. Let's get started, shall we?"

Low Level Whiners

I don't advise you deal with these people at all. But, if something does go wrong and you find yourself boxed in, here's a quick technique to extricate yourself. The key is, to deliver it with conviction and authority; you are in charge of this evaluation and of your company's resources, too. Don't let yourself get bullied into spending them in a way that doesn't help you. So, when they say;

Why can't we just get a proposal and make a decision on it?

"Can we be honest? We aren't a real contender here for you, are we?"

No, not the way the others are.

"I understand John. Not everyone wants to do business the way we've decided to do it. Why don't we save some time and stop now?"

Know that not everyone is going to buy from you. Not everyone that you get into the Momentum step will end up moving past the Audit. You must have a way of dividing non-prospects from you at your own initiative, or they will separate themselves from you at a later stage after you have invested a tremendous amount of time and effort.

Chapter 32: **Building a Business Case**

What is the MAJOR™ Justify Stage?

The MAJOR™ Justify Stage is a meeting where you present a Business Case for your solution. It is a meeting where you present a reason for buying your solution based on information you gleaned from the prospect during the Audit.

- The Justify Stage is about setting the Stage for a Proposal
- Showing your Findings from the Audit
- Presenting Options for Solving their Problem
- The Prospect Chooses an Option to Pursue
- You Leave to Design a Proposal Around that Option.

Why Use the MAJOR™ Justify Stage

The Justify Stage allows for mutual qualification. The prospect wants to know things like you understand their problem; you are capable of solving their problem and can demonstrate that empathy as an expert who is capable of solving the problem.

For your part, you want to ensure you are not caught up in wasted time writing proposals for a prospect who is not really interested; you want to be sure all your sales issues receive the proper attention, including that there is budget for the solution, the incumbent is not an automatic choice and why and that the prospect is ultimately trustworthy.

Using the Justify Stage gives you more time with your prospect as you work through scenarios of your solution and its potential positive impact on the prospect's environment. This type of interaction is the stuff of which great business relationships are made.

Additionally, the Justify Stage is a great margin-maker. Presenting options for how much savings or how much earnings can be made with your solution keeps the focus off of how much margin they would like removed from your *price.* The focus is on what the potential return of your solution is and less on what the actual price of the solution is. In this way, your own business case is the determinant of the validity of your price, rather than whatever cheap price your competition might be offering.

Finally, the Justify Stage give you an opportunity to understand what needs to go into a proposal and to do so with a room full of the ultimate decision makers who themselves would never attend a proposal presentation, but will make time for an expert presenting options to improve their business.

Ultimately, the Justify Stage will put fun and ease into your sales cycle—there is nothing like being able to show a credible business case which makes your prospect look stupid for not buying it.

Overcoming a Huge Sales-Killer!

Lots of salespeople want to present their own version of a proposal here, way too fast. They argue that the prospect needs to see the pricing and 'how it all works.' No, the prospect doesn't need anything like that.

In the end, you need to know that the prospect doesn't start caring about your price until you let him.

Until then, all he cares about is his return. If he feels comfortable he is going to make a million dollars from a $100,000 investment, he is going to make the investment.

If he feels that the above applies, but the salesperson is willing to 'talk about price' then the feeding frenzy begins. Realize the costs to your prospect of engaging in a discount war--if you discount your service a huge 30%, you have just taken his million-dollar return up a lousy 3%. That's three percent!

You may argue that they don't really believe they're going to save a million dollars, that it's easier for them to see the price reduction and that's why the discount is important. Rubbish! They don't need to save money on anything that they do not already believe is going to add huge value to them—if they did not believe it was going to add huge value, the best way to save money would be not to spend it in the first place.

So don't believe for one second that they're willing to buy something that they don't think is going to help them. They only declare open season on your pricing when you let them know that you view your list pricing as 'sucker's pricing.' Avoid this by standing firm and selling the value of the return on their money.

That's why the Justify step is so important.

Business Case versus a Proposal

How does a business case differ from a proposal?

- A business case makes broad claims as to the prospect's gains from using it; a proposal lays out the specific terms of acquiring that solution.
- A business case begins with a description of the benefits to the prospect; the proposal ends with pricing terms and conditions.
- The business case is never binding; the proposal is often legal and binding.
- The business case focuses on several possible options; the proposal should be focused on a single option.

And finally, the business case is customer-centric in that it is concerned mainly with what the experience of the customer of the solution will be; the proposal tends to be more of a Seller's document in that it specifies terms of acquisition that protect the Seller from loss.

Planning

If you have a multi-member sales team for the opportunity, get your sales team together before this meeting, as this is the big-show as far as team presentation and cooperation are involved. More than any other stage, your team needs to choreograph your involvement carefully and exactly. Remember, this is a presentation, not a free for all.

CLIENT Map™

Spend time on each of the CLIENT™ issues you want to know more of; issues that are still outstanding and are unanswered; and those items which you will need to get reconfirmed. Compile a list of questions and an agenda for the meeting.

Meeting Plan

Using a Meeting Plan starting on page 18 of the CLIENT Map™ will ensure you are fully prepared.

After the Meeting

After the meeting, return to your CLIENT Map™ and fill in the answers.

Format Your Business Case

Formatting your business case properly will give maximum impact in your presentation.

Options

Use their data you have picked up from the Audit and apply it to a few scenarios or options. Include customers who have experienced these benefits in similar industries. Focus on summarizing each scenario with bottom line benefits;

- Reduce Overhead 35%
- Cut Time to Market 65%
- Increase Profits 20%
- Throughput Up 80%
- Improve Quality 22%

Use PowerPoint®

There is nothing like the impact of your information when you can show the prospect's process and his problem and then show a solution scenario where he will save hundreds of thousands if not millions; all on one screen for the whole group of decision makers.

Hand-Outs

Leave copies of the presentation in the form of handouts *behind* for anyone who was not at the presentation. Certain members of the group will certainly continue the discussions after you have left and this information will of course be helpful.

A Sample Discussion Track using CLIENT™

Commitment

Introduce your Agenda for the meeting. Read through it out loud and ask if anyone wants to add anything to it. Pause just long enough for someone to speak, someone who has something to say on the tip of his or her tongue. If you wait any longer you'll invite the kind of help that you don't want.

Review why you're here. Let them know that you've done a study of their environment and found some areas of improvement. Explain that these results are reliable and that you will show them the basis for that reliability. Also, explain that this is not the time for final decisions on their part, because that time will come only after you have proved your claims in the proposal.

Leadership

Confirm the stakeholders' identities. Yes, you just went through a whole lot to identify who these people are in the Audit step. What you're going to do here, is confirm--in the presence of everyone attending this meeting--that you got your facts right. You'll go around the table again, just like you did in preceding meetings, only this time you're going to confirm with the key players *what* they're here to see. Don't worry about making an incorrect statement; they will correct you.

Impact

Confirm that the problems that you've selected to go over are the correct problems. Pause to makes sure everyone is on board.

Show the top problems. Again, close to ensure that everyone is on board.

Economics

Show the accuracy of your ROI (Return on Investment.)

Be sure that you have not inserted anything about NPV, IRR, Discount Rates, Cost of Capital, etc. Every company has their own way of handling this data and since it ties into their vital signs, they are understandably very sensitive to it.

Additionally, it's a thousand times easier to be wrong about these numbers than it is to be right so don't reach for the stars by showing how hopelessly inadequate you are as a financial analyst. Focus instead on keeping to the nuts and bolts of your solutions specific areas of improvement. *They* will take those improvement numbers and add all the relevant financial statistics to it afterwards, with the net result is that your assumed ROI will only increase in perceived value.

Confirm that the ROI is acceptable. Of course, to do the ROI correctly you have to know what you are going to charge them in terms of pricing. Do not go into detailed pricing for them; a lump sum investment works just fine for your purposes here. The reason is simple. If you detail your solutions proposal you'll be spending all of your time talking about the various inputs and outputs and options available on that proposal. They will pound you with questions about what can they "get away with to start."

Explain what your position is on pricing and discounting. If you have authority for discounting, describe that; if there's a policy for discounting describe it. Sometimes this can help you close the deal. In other words, when you discount, how do you do it? When I sold software years ago, I used to say that there were two ways to get a discount from me. They had to do with timing and volume respectively. That is if they bought from me within this time period--usually this quarter-- I could have some flexibility. If they bought a higher volume when they bought, I had more flexibility. When you explain it like this, you add credence and credibility to your pricing policies.

Confirm that budget is available to solve this problem.

Need

Confirm that you have identified the Specification Rules correctly and that nothing stands in the way of purchase if everyone in the room agrees.

You confirmed that budget is available; now confirm it is under what conditions? What would need to be demonstrated—to be proven—to access that budget? How do they determine the worthiness of a particular project for receiving funds?

Review the requirements that you've collected up to this point—be sure it's correct.

If you perform test evaluations, begin to frame the test requirements.

Clarify any ambiguities. For instance, if everyone has to provide three references persuade the prospect to apply specific controls to the reference. Point out that every reference they check will be a positive reference; would a vendor be expected to submit a bad one? So, what is the process for making sure they get the same high quality information from each reference check? Make a suggestion to them that they develop a questionnaire and that they take each reference through it. Mark check boxes and specifics next to each. Have a 'Duration of Call' entry. If they don't have one, offer a template.

If you get resistance to this, ask;

- ✓ "Why? What's wrong with making the decision visible, so you can inspect it and be sure that you made the right one?"

Be sure that even if there is a competing salesperson that has the edge that this document is not going to help him.

TimeLine

Confirm the date for the test or proposal. Also, find out whether or not anything has come up on the company timeline that might impact their ability to implement a decision in the foreseeable future.

Problems and Objections

Problems and objections in the Justify stage are largely in the form of attacks on the validity of your conclusions. These are real easy to defend, since in the Audit, they gave you the information that you based your assumptions upon. The only thing you would have added is what your solution does for them, which only you, as that solution's expert, are equipped to validate. If your conclusions are inaccurate, then it will be because they gave you incorrect information in the first place.

Chapter 33: **Proposals**

The MAJOR™ Offer Stage

You will deliver the proposal in this the fourth stage of the MAJOR™ Sales Process, making your value now in the form of an Offer.

What is a Proposal?

The proposal is a document that lists the type, nature and quantity of your solution with the price to be paid by the prospect to buy it.

The proposal is the most important document you will submit to your prospect other than your contracts.

The Key to Writing Winning Proposals

The key to writing a winning proposal is designing it so that it sells to someone you may never meet, who has very limited time and even less technical aptitude to appreciate your solutions features, who doesn't like details and is both highly and expertly skeptical.

How to Deliver a Proposal

In person, by you. You earn the right to do this by not submitting any proposal unless you oversee the first such review of it for the good of everyone involved.

Proposals that Fail

Failed proposals can be an excellent source of instruction for salespeople.

When Proposals Fail

Proposals fail all the time, due to the ignorance of the writer, the reader or both.

- Proposals fail when the prospect does not get what he wants, namely when the proposal does not prove all the great claims made by the salesperson up to that point.
- The Proposal fails when the salesperson doesn't get what he wants and is forced to focus on price and discounts rather than the value of his solution.
- Proposals fail when the CEO or CFO or some other C-level executive assumes control, reads the proposals and is unclear or unconvinced about why his company should spend so much money on something which he cannot understand.
- Proposals fail mostly because salespeople do not know that a proposal is only about proving claims about their solution's business impact to a business decision maker whom they probably will never meet.

How Proposals Fail: Mutual Misconceptions

Proposals fail when they're based on mutual misconceptions.

For the Salesperson;

- The salesperson views the proposal as a simple formality prior to the prospect purchasing. He thinks the prospect will read all the information, and will either understand the information as it is presented or will contact the salesperson and ask questions if he is unclear about anything.
- The salesperson believes the decision makers who read the proposal are known by the salesperson or will be at some point; and that they are forgiving of unclear assertions in the proposal; that they are unbiased and that they are all ready to sign the check for the solution.

For the Prospect;

- The prospect thinks the proposal will show the *starting* or asking price of the solution, pricing which will certainly come down when the prospect needs it to.
- The prospect believes the proposal should address all questions which were previously unanswered.
- The prospect thinks the proposal should *begin* the process of internal analysis and debate over the solution, which of course will be considered alongside other competitive solutions. He believes the proposal will lead to more serious discussion with the salesperson—when the prospect is good and ready to do so.

- The prospect believes that the proposal is an important step that may—possibly—perhaps—potentially—one day lead to a purchase.

Designing a Proposal

The Proposal is Proof

What is Proof?

- Proof is reliable evidence.
- Proof is a good business case.
- Proof is validated claims with references as to success in other customers with similar if not identical environments and who had similar if not identical needs.
- Proof is when the prospect can enjoy shared internal support; a consensus among his peers and the executives of his own company as to the viability of your solution.
- Proof is when your proposal presents a sensible summary of all of these elements.

How Do You Get Proof?

You've got it.

- ✓ You promised the world in your First Meeting.
- ✓ You studied—as an expert—their own situation in the Audit.
- ✓ You presented options—as an expert—in your business case in the Justify Stage.
- ✓ Now, you need to propose it—as an expert—making it "Obvious."

What to Include in Your Proposal

What should you include in your proposal?

- ✓ Everything you believe is needed to sell to someone you may never meet.
- ✓ Straightforward Pricing, not complicated options and sub-options that might even confuse the pricing people at your own company.
- ✓ ROI—the return on investment which you presented in the Justify stage should be also included here, with any enhancements or adjustments as needed.
- ✓ References, successes of those customers having a similarity to the prospect considering your offer.
- ✓ Highlighted Terms, especially if these are a unique and beneficial offer to this particular prospect.
- ✓ Contracts and any explanation of special terms.
- ✓ An Expiration Date for the proposal (they do not have forever to decide.)
- ✓ One Page Executive Summary (for that unseen, unfamiliar executive.)

What Should Be Left Out of Your Proposal

These items should be left out of your proposal.

- Basic Sales Literature; you've got the best information possible—theirs—so leave the generics out.
- Complex Pricing Schemes; if you try to use complexity to convince the prospect of the intelligence behind your solution, you run the risk of confusing them into believing your competitor's simpler proposal is proof of their superior solution.
- Discounts; do not show discounts unless you absolutely have to.
- Obvious Sales Language

- Typos, Misspellings; show your intelligence and understanding of the most basic tools you used to create the proposal by running the spellchecker before you publish it.
- Customers Name from Last Proposal You Wrote (find & replace); it's amazing how often this happens to careless salespeople who simply replace the names (they think) of the customer they last created a proposal for. It only takes one slip to blow that big deal; instead make your proposals exercises in personalization.

Two Types of Readers

You will find there are two basic types of readers of your proposals; the patient reader who will review your proposals exactly as they are laid out, from the front cover to the last page.

The other type is the attention-challenged reader who will rip directly to the page they hope to find the information they want to read and will base their entire impression of the worth of your proposal based on what they find there.

Most salespeople prepare for the patient reader, even though they know he is very rare.

Be ready for both, by laying out your proposal in a logical fashion, but include instructions as to where to find the information that the attention-challenged reader really wants.

Readability

Make your proposal readable by reducing or eliminating buzzwords—explain your solution benefits in plain terms that the non-technical business decision maker will understand when he reads it. The only exception to this is when your

Audit has uncovered special terms used inside their own company; in that case use them liberally, being first double-sure of their meaning and that they are well understood and used inside the company.

Use color-coding for different sections, or pages. By highlighting sections with red, blue or green you can improve the comprehension of your reader considerably over black and white text. Give this consideration, especially if your proposals tend to run more than a few pages.

Know Your Prospect

Often, your prospect can feel like a rat in a maze, chasing after the cheese and frustrated with every corner he has to turn to find it. Where is your customer's cheese? The answer is where they go first in your proposal.

- Where do your prospects go first?
- Why do they go there first?
- Where do they go next?

For many prospects, the pricing page is the cheese; that's all they want and when they find it, they're done with reading.

How do you get them to the cheese in your way? How can you get them to review your proposal and come away having spent time on the pages you really wanted them to spend time on?

The key is in knowing the pages they will be reading and then getting them from those pages to the others.

Three Pages They Always Read

If you are not sure what your prospect will tend to read first, you can fall back to leveraging the pages that he will *always* read. There are three pages they always read, no matter what.

- ✓ Cover (always)
- ✓ Pricing Page (always)
- ✓ First Page (often)

They always read the cover page, the pricing page and often, they read the first inside page. These pages are the key to setting up your Value Maze.

The Value Maze

The Value Maze is the order in which you guide them through your proposal, starting with what they want to know and leading them to where you want them.

For instance, if your Competitive Analysis is where you want them to go and if they shoot straight for the pricing page first, you need to have some way to get them over to where you want them.

Building the Value Maze

The key to constructing the Value Maze is to understand what the prospect wants out of your proposal and what you want him to know. What will prospect want to consider;

1. First
2. Next
3. Last, only if he has time?

Take a look at one of your own proposals. What order is it in? What does the prospect see first and is that what you want him to see first? Now, think about what *you* want the prospect to consider;

1. Foremost
2. Second
3. Third

You may want your prospect to read your introduction, then your competitive analysis and finally your pricing. Your prospect may prefer to read your pricing and—if that looks good—your competitive analysis.

Breadcrumbs

If you know the pricing page is the first stop for your prospects you can place a textbox breadcrumb on that page and direct them to a page they wouldn't otherwise visit. A page you know would help them to appreciate your value if only you could get them to read it. Place a textbox in the margin like;

- WARNING! see page 4
- ATTENTION: see page 7
- How Can We Do This? See page 2
- How we got here: see pg. 1
- The Money-Maker: see ROI pg. 8

Make them noticeable and irresistible; use bold formatting and color to get your page visited. Text box messages which say things like this will considerably increase the chance that your time sensitive reader will take the time to bounce back from his page of highest interest and give the other pages of your proposal more attention.

There are a few rules of text boxes;

- Do use them
- Do not overuse them; limit your use to 2 to 3. Overuse can be plain confusing.
- Use formatting to grab attention, but be careful not to overdo the formatting. Too much formatting can clash and create visual distractions. Be aware that just the presence of your textboxes will be new and attention grabbing.

Your Proposal Cover

Another place you want to give attention to is your cover. What does it look like now? Probably has a company logo, a big, bold, dead title, a date and your name. For one of the pages they are sure to read, that isn't exactly leveraging their attention to your advantage.

Now see if you can look around and find a magazine cover. Notice how the publishers do not take for granted that you are going to open and read it? You can see how they have placed appealing and attention grabbing titles with page references for you to quickly jump to. They know if they can get you moving around inside, they will stand a much better chance of getting exposure to the advertisers who have bought space in their pages; maybe you'll even buy something. Isn't the goal of your proposal exactly the same?

What can you do with your cover to ensure your key pages get read? Try some catchy subtitles in text boxes;

"You Won't Believe This…Page 3"

"CFO's LOVE this fact about our solution…page 4, item 12"

A Final Word on Proposals

You have worked hard to get to the point where you can present a proposal; keep up the good work and this prospect will soon be a customer.

Planning the MAJOR™ Offer Meeting

You should take the time to thoroughly plan out the MAJOR™ Offer step as with all your previous steps. Use the available ScoreSelling™ tools such as CLIENT™ Map.

CLIENT Map™

Before the meeting, conduct a strategy session both by yourself and with your team, including your Sales Manager. Spend time on each of the CLIENT™ issues you want to know more of. Compile a list of questions and an agenda for the meeting.

Meeting Plan

Using a Meeting Plan starting on page 19 of the CLIENT Map™ will ensure you are fully prepared.

After the Meeting

After the meeting, return to your CLIENT Map™ and fill in the answers.

Chapter 34: **Closing**

The MAJOR™ Revenue Stage

What is the Revenue Stage?

The MAJOR™ Revenue Stage is the conclusion of the sales process. It is a meeting to negotiate any final terms, sign contracts and collect payment.

Misconceptions

Misconceptions abound regarding the end of the sales cycle and the need for the salesperson to be a closer. However, hard closing is not necessary in the Revenue Stage. The MAJOR™ sales process has built enough buyer's equity for your solution so that hard closing should not be necessary.

Buyers Equity (CLIENT™) in the MAJOR™ Revenue Stage

Building Buyer's Equity in the Revenue Stage is accomplished by courteous negotiating through reminding the prospect of the value your solution will bring to him. Negotiation should have been done in degrees and throughout the sales process by this point, but sometimes the prospect will attempt to get your price down anyway. In this case, simply hold your ground, review how you got here with appropriate documentation, restate your desire to do business and ask to get started.

Discounter's Warning!

A 30% discount off a $100k price, which has a $1 million ROI to prospect, adds only 3% to his gain---AND KILLS YOUR MARGIN!

How to Say No

Here is one way to handle it when the prospect says, "Lower your price."

Refuse

"No.."

Regret

"I'm sorry I can't do that…"

Reaffirm

"But, I'd really like to do business with you…"

Request

"How do we make that happen?"

Other Types of Pressure

Sometimes the prospect will use other means to apply pressure, some of them obvious, others are less conspicuous. Some of them are designed to scare you into believing your price is too high; others are meant to make you feel good about lowering your price and helping them out. All of them are intended to take margin from your solution and add it to their cost savings.

Aggressive

"You're too expensive!"

You fail this test if you respond with; "If we discount it more, would you consider us?"

You pass with something like "We may not be the fit for you."

Confusion

"I'm not sure where that leaves us?"

You Fail with a response like "We can fix that—what do we need to do?"

You Pass by saying something like "What is it that's confusing you?"

Flattery

"You must be your company's top salesman!"

You fail if you say, "Gee, thanks, I hope to be someday…"

You pass when you say, "It's my responsibility to ensure you're taken care of."

Pressure Conclusion

Successfully exiting a pressure situation means you have taken the heat off of your price, the attention off of yourself and returned to the discussion.

Planning the MAJOR™ Revenue Meeting

You should take the time to thoroughly plan out the MAJOR™ Revenue Stage as with all your previous stages. Use the available ScoreSelling™ tools.

CLIENT Map™

Before the meeting, conduct a strategy session both by yourself and with your team, including your Sales Manager. Develop a plan to handle any of the CLIENT™ issues that may need attention. Especially;

- ✓ Is the prospect prepared to close the order today?
- ✓ Are key decision makers planning on attending the meeting?

Meeting Plan

Using a Meeting Plan starting on page 20 of the CLIENT Map™ will ensure you are fully prepared.

After the Meeting

After the meeting, return to your CLIENT Map™ and fill in the answers.

A Sample CLIENT™ Discussion Track

Agenda Outline

Layout a simple agenda outline that looks something like this;

- o How We Got Here
- o Where We're Going
- o Review
  - What It Costs
  - What It Saves
  - What's the Risk
  - Where's the Proof
- o What We Do Now
  - Why We Should Not Wait

Commitment

Confirm that your prospect is ready to approve the deal based upon acceptable contracts & pricing. Get the contract paperwork into their hands as soon as possible. Especially if their legal department has to review them.

Step through the above agenda for the meeting and close for acceptance.

Leadership

You will want to make sure that nobody on your paper path has taken a vacation or is otherwise occupied. Verify that your requisition has traveled the entire paper path and isn't held up anywhere.

Impact

At any point in the Revenue step, be ready to produce your documentation on your ROI and proposal.

The main thing you do is to keep their interest in moving ahead. How long can they go with the problems remaining unsolved? The prospect always seems to forget this during this final stage; be sure that you serve the vital role of helping them to remember.

Economics

Eventually there will be the subject of pricing and your willingness to discount. Be smart about it and be ready for it. When the prospect says 'I think the price is the problem' you need to be able to say 'I disagree; unless you don't think the ROI is real.' By doing this, you will keep the attention focused on the real issue—solving their multi million dollar business problem.

Throughout this final negotiating process remember these words. "I'm sorry I can't do that; but I *really* want to do business with you. How can we get this done?" Do not break this statement apart; say it altogether. Amazingly, this simple statement both shows the prospect how tough you are on price, but simultaneously braces his ego up by reaffirming that you want his business. It is incredible how effective this disarming, even charming statement will be in your negotiating technique.

Need

Confirm that your implementation schedule is acceptable.

TimeLine

Sign the contracts and pick up the check or purchase order.

Sample Negotiating and Saying "No"

"I really want to do business with you, how can we make that happen?"

Well, lower your price 20%.

"No, I'm sorry I can't do that; but I'd really like to do business with you how can we get this done?"

Well, meet me in the middle; how about lowering your price 10% or 15%?

"No, I'm sorry I can't do that; but I'd love to do business with you; how can we get this done?"

Look, you've got to meet me somewhere. What kind of a discount can you give me?

"Bill, I'm not sure where this is coming from now. I respect your position though; if you cannot do business with me you can just let me know. Is that the case?"

No it's not the case. I just need you to meet me somewhere. I need to have little bit of a win here. Honestly, toss me a bone kid. Show me that you want my business.

[Bring out your documentation.]

"I appreciate you allowing me a chance to show you again how much I want your business. Is this ROI correct?"

You mean, do I know that you're going to save me $1.2 million? Honestly I don't think it's going to be that much.

"You don't? How much do you think?"

Look, I know where you're going. This isn't about anything we've already talked about. This is how much you've asked me to pay. Work with me on this price.

"No, I'm sorry I can't do that; and now I'm starting to get concerned about something."

What are you getting concerned about?

"That my value did not come through to you. That you don't believe the $1.2 million I'm going to save you is real. If it did register with you, a man in your position would not be arguing points off the basic investment; he'd be more interested in making sure that I delivered 100% on the return."

All I want is a few points discounted and we'll call it a done deal. We're talking about $100,000.00 here, right? Knock off a few points and let's get going.

"If I knocked off 10%, that would add less than 1% to your overall ROI. Right?"

To $1.2 million? Yes, that would be right.

"And the reason you want me to do that is probably because that $1.2 million doesn't appear real to you."

No, it does; it might even be more. I want you to show me some flexibility in your pricing as my prospective partner.

"I'm just not going to do that sir. Every step of the way in this process, as John will testify, I have put all my focus and energy into making sure that you folks knew, beyond a shadow of a doubt, that we're going to be a great solution for you."

And that's why you're here.

"And that's exactly why I am not willing to compromise that now--by knocking off a few points that doesn't make any difference anyway, just to get a deal--when I need to be more concerned about you as my customer. I am not a desperate salesman, and I don't like looking like one. You're way too important to me. You deserve way better."

[Pause.]

We're not going to be an easy customer you know. We're going to demand that you deliver exactly what you said you would deliver.

"I believe that, sir. That's why I believe you're going to be a great reference for me. That's why I really want to do business with you."

I'm not kidding. We will be a great reference for you, but you have to perform. No ifs, ands or buts.

"I understand sir. Let's do it."

Have we got absolutely everything we need in this document? Then, let's get this done.

"Thank you, Bill. I look forward to working with you and your fine organization."

Summary

You can see several points where most of us would be tempted to jump in and say OK here is your 10% discount; let's do the deal. And that is your choice if you think that is going to work for you. It is, of course, an extreme example of holding out on your price. But I make this example to illustrate something vital. If you have done your job and carried out the sales process and have distributed the best information you could so that they could make the best decision possible, there is nothing to gain by buckling on price. In fact, there is a lot to lose by doing just that; because you will be stepping out of character with the prospect. You will cease to be the value added consultant and suddenly appear as the salesman. Be careful how you handle this part of the process.

Chapter 35: Customer Service and Referrals

Taking Care of Your Customers

What is Customer Service

Don't get fancy—just make sure they're well cared for.

Why?

Taking care of your customers is a reflection of your own honor and integrity—take care of them and you show you've got both qualities working for you.

Building customer loyalty is a great way to ensure your customers will come back to buy from you and buy more when they do buy.

You can significantly reduce your prospecting costs by selling to your existing customers. Not only that but you can generate a list of high quality referrals to help in your prospecting efforts.

Finally, it's a lot easier and less expensive to keep a new customer than to try and replace him.

Handling Disaster

Mistakes happen. What do you do when they happen to you and your service?

First off, you take responsibility—do not pass the buck. As a company and as a salesperson, taking responsibility is of primary importance and will immediately give your customer a sense that the problem is sure to be resolved. Passing the buck only infuriates them, gives them a sense that the problem may not be resolved and ultimately has them shopping a replacement for your service at their earliest opportunity.

Fix the problem!

Keep in touch throughout the correction progress with consistent updates, even if there isn't much to update them on. Keep the lines of communication open so that they know you are dealing with the problem.

Schedule a review after the problem is corrected and take them through how you have corrected the issue. You should bring someone like your head of customer service, or your sales manager. Be sure they know that the problem they had is being viewed as a problem and that you have taken steps to avoid in the future.

Provide some extras in the form of service freebies; lunches or something of value to the prospect that says that you understand the issue was an inconvenience.

Fact

Problems are opportunities to strengthen the relationship!

Proactive Customer Service

Do you know why your customers bought from your company? Sometimes you may inherit customers without knowing their history up-close and personal. Take the time to call a meeting with these customers and find out;

- ✓ How they buy
- ✓ What they need
- ✓ When they need it
- ✓ Why do they buy from you?

How to Find Out

Schedule customer-reviews by setting;

- ✓ Meetings
- ✓ Luncheons

Making a review request

"Customer satisfaction is vital to me and I am always interested in professional improvement. Would you be willing to review my performance with me?"

Sure

"How about lunch this Thursday?"

If

- No, not over lunch or
- No, not Thursday

Ask

"OK—when, then?"

Time Saving Tips for Proactive Customer Service

Nighttime Voicemails: you can leave messages for your customer after hours and let them know you are thinking about them. You can take 60 minutes and leave 15-20 voicemails if you plan your time right. That way you're not caught up in conversations if that is not your goal right now.

You can also make calls anytime you might have a break, in drive time, waiting rooms, etc.

If appropriate, you can either drop off small gifts of cookies or candy or have them dropped off by a service.

Getting Referrals

What is a Referral?

A referral is a personal introduction to a prospect from an existing customer. Consumer salespeople consider referrals from family, friends, peers and acquaintances. For your purposes, you should focus on referrals from your existing customers.

Why Do You Want a Referral?

You will enjoy a shorter time involved in closing new business because referrals to qualified prospects will save you the time of having to go and find the qualified prospect on your own. Also you will find;

- ✓ Higher Success Rate in Closing
- ✓ Less Proposals Wasted
- ✓ Easier Access
- ✓ Less Cold Calling

Why Referrals Work

When the business prospect is faced with a major purchase there is a certain amount of fear, uncertainty and doubt. Getting a referral from a trusted resource can help offset this.

The Number One Reason Referrals Are Given

The number one reason referrals are given is to make the referrer look good. That is, to make the person who gives the referral look smart, sophisticated or in some way put them in a good light.

A distant second reason is to benefit the person to whom the referral is given.

Think about the last time you referred a friend to a movie, or to a restaurant and you will see that it had as much to do with earning their respect and regard as it was to give them some kind of benefit.

It will help you as a salesperson when you request referrals if you keep in mind these top two reasons. And where is the concern over the salesperson and giving referrals to a salesperson in order to benefit him? Sure, it happens, but not enough to count on it.

Three Ways to Ask for Referrals

Work the request into your customer service routine and you will be way ahead of the game.

Don't Try This

"Would you be willing to help me out?"

Or,

"I do everything by relationships. Who do you know in your company who handles…"?

Try This

"One of my professional objectives is to find contacts that are simply aware of what it is I do. Would you know of someone in the organization I might provide information to?"

Keep It Simple

(You saw this in the Customer Service section.)

- "Customer satisfaction is vital to me and I am always interested in professional improvement. Would you be willing to review my performance with me?
    - *Sure*
- "How about lunch this Thursday?"
- If
    - *No, not over lunch* or *No, not Thursday*
- Ask
    - "OK—when, then?"

Example Opener 1

Once you are at the luncheon, get the ball rolling on the referral process.

- "One of the ways I gauge satisfaction is to simply ask;"
- "Would you refer someone to me?"

Or

- "In your opinion, is there merit in letting "X" department know who we are for any future needs they may have?"

Example Opener 2

Use the following to open the referral discussion softly.

- ✓ "Word of mouth is our preferred way of finding new customers;"
- ✓ "Would you be willing to act as a reference for us if I had someone who wanted to talk with a previous customer?"
- ✓ "Would you feel comfortable referring me to someone YOU know?"

Starting the Referral Process with a Brand New Customer

This version of the referral request is performed at the beginning of the customer relationship, when the customer-honeymoon is in full bloom.

- "One key differentiator is for you to know right now---that I will be working to earn your recommendation to others through the quality of work we do for you."
- "When we do that, will you have any problem recommending me to someone else--at the end of this project?"

OK.

- "The way you answered that sounds as if you're thinking of someone in particular already?"

Yes, his name is John Doe at XYZ Corp. You should call on him—want his info?

In this way, you can get some excellent referrals right upfront in your customer relationship.

Objection

Customer says;

- *I don't really know about other projects…*
- "How about someone in a similar position as yourself?"
- *I do, but I don't know if he has a project coming up…*
- "Maybe he might be willing to receive information from me from time to time?"
- *Yeah, I guess that would be fine. Would you like his contact info?*

When You Get a Referral

Act on it now!

Some salespeople like to put the referral on the shelf, saving it for that "rainy day." Referrals have a shelf life for good reason—suppose your customer runs into the referral and asks if he's heard from you? Not a situation you want to be in.

Additionally, when you make contact with the referral, call the person who gave you the referral and let them know that you made contact with them and what you'll be doing next. Also, once the referral either buys or doesn't buy, call the person who gave you the referral and let them know how things turned out; least take them to lunch to thank them. The worst insult to a referrer is to find out from the referral that he's been doing business with you for some time because you have not had the courtesy to let him know that. Be the first one to tell your referrer the outcome of his valuable referral to you and this will never happen to you.

Part VIII: Final Word

Chapter 36: **Use It**

You've completed the ScoreSelling™ 3.0 book.

Great start!

Now Use It

Put it to work. The difference between success and failure is execution, effort and consistency.

Let me know how it's going for you.

May God bless you.

Index

